Collins

citizenship today

for Edexcel GCSE

Jenny Wales

William Collins' dream of knowledge for all began with the publication of his first book in 1819. A self-educated mill worker, he not only enriched millions of lives, but also founded a flourishing publishing house. Today, staying true to this spirit, Collins books are packed with inspiration, innovation and practical expertise. They place you at the centre of a world of possibility and give you exactly what you need to explore it.

Collins. Freedom to teach.

An imprint of HarperCollins*Publishers*
The News Building
1 London Bridge Street
London
SE1 9GF

browse the complete Collins catalogue at
www.collins.co.uk

ISBN 978-0-00-816292-4

Jenny Wales asserts her moral right to be identified as the author of this work.

British Library Cataloguing in Publication Data
A catalogue record for this publication is available from the British Library.

Commissioning editors Tom Guy and Cathy Martin
Managing editor Caroline Green
Project managed by Emily Hooton
Edited by Jo Kemp
Proofread by Trish Chapman
Cover design by Ink Tank Associates
Cover image Anna Omelchenko/Shutterstock
Internal design and typesetting by Ken Vail Graphic Design
Permissions research by Rachel Thorne
Picture research by Suzanne Williams
Illustrations by Jennifer Skemp – Advocate Art
Production by Rachel Weaver

Printed and bound by Grafica Veneta S. P. A.

With special thanks to Christian Borresen of Ashcroft Academy, Putney.

Endorsement Statement

In order to ensure that this resource offers high-quality support for the associated Pearson qualification, it has been through a review process by the awarding body. This process confirms that this resource fully covers the teaching and learning content of the specification or part of a specification at which it is aimed. It also confirms that it demonstrates an appropriate balance between the development of subject skills, knowledge and understanding, in addition to preparation for assessment.

Endorsement does not cover any guidance on assessment activities or processes (e.g. practice questions or advice on how to answer assessment questions), included in the resource nor does it prescribe any particular approach to the teaching or delivery of a related course.

While the publishers have made every attempt to ensure that advice on the qualification and its assessment is accurate, the official specification and associated assessment guidance materials are the only authoritative source of information and should always be referred to for definitive guidance.

Pearson examiners have not contributed to any sections in this resource relevant to examination papers for which they have responsibility.

Examiners will not use endorsed resources as a source of material for any assessment set by Pearson.

Endorsement of a resource does not mean that the resource is required to achieve this Pearson qualification, nor does it mean that it is the only suitable material available to support the qualification, and any resource lists produced by the awarding body shall include this and other appropriate resources.

Contents

Theme D Power and influence

Theme E Taking Citizenship action

How to use this book

The *Citizenship Today Student Book* follows the five themes of Edexcel's Citizenship GCSE. Each chapter offers lessons covering all the content you will need for your course.

Engaging starting points introduce each topic

Contemporary case studies bring different aspects of each topic to life

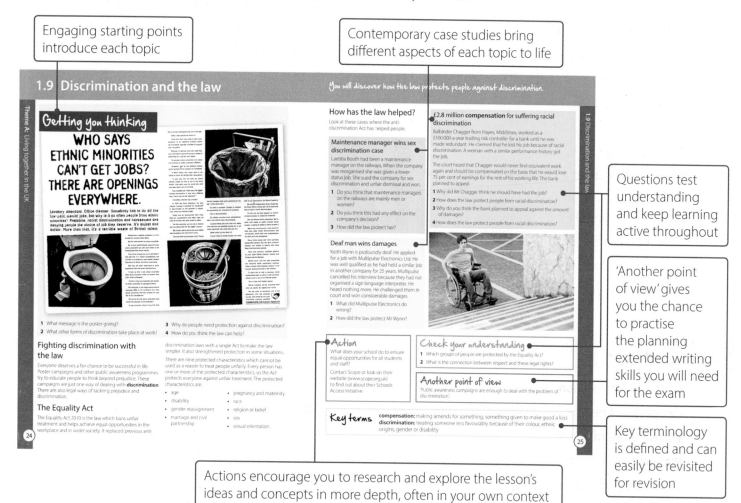

Questions test understanding and keep learning active throughout

'Another point of view' gives you the chance to practise the planning extended writing skills you will need for the exam

Key terminology is defined and can easily be revisited for revision

Actions encourage you to research and explore the lesson's ideas and concepts in more depth, often in your own context

At the end of each chapter you will have the opportunity to apply your knowledge and skills to a range of practice questions, and to explore annotated sample responses to these questions.

Please note: these sections do not provide complete practice assessments but simply offer a flavour of the types of question that you may meet in your examinations.

Practice questions give you the opportunity to apply your learning

Student answers with commentary show you how to apply the skills and knowledge from each chapter and suggest how your work could be improved

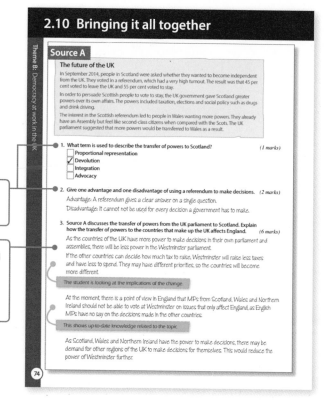

Living together in the UK

1.1 What is a community?

Getting you thinking

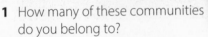

1 How many of these communities do you belong to?

2 What other communities do you belong to?

3 How many of these communities do you share with people of different ages and/or interests?

4 If you don't belong to some of these communities, do you know people who do? How do you know these people?

5 What do these communities give you and what do you give them?

Belonging to a community

A **community** is a group of people who are connected in some way. Most people belong to several communities. Someone your age, living in the UK, could be a member of all the following communities and others: school, the local neighbourhood, the country, the European Union and a religious group.

Neighbourhoods

There is a lot of overlap between different communities.

A **neighbourhood** community refers to a group of people who share local interests because of where they live.

It might be the whole of a village or small town, but in a city the neighbourhood can be more difficult to identify. For example, someone living in Whitechapel in London might think of their neighbourhood as 'London', 'Whitechapel', 'the East End' or even just their own particular street.

You will discover the meaning of community and understand how you can belong to more than one community at the same time.

'I belong to...'

As well as belonging to a neighbourhood, people are also connected by their lifestyle, religion, ethnicity or nationality.

The Chinese community

The Chinese community in the UK dates back to the mid-1800s. Members of the Chinese community live in all parts of the UK and there are well-established 'Chinatowns' in Birmingham, Liverpool, London, Manchester and Newcastle. There are over 400 Chinese organisations that serve the needs of the Chinese community in the UK, including language schools, women's groups, and art and business associations. Chinese New Year, food, martial arts, medicine and Feng Shui have all become part of British life.

The Christian community

There are almost 49,000 Christian churches in the United Kingdom across more than 10 different denominations, ranging from Church of England and Roman Catholic to Methodist and Greek Orthodox. As well as involving people in the wider Christian community, many churches are a focus for local people, offering facilities and events to Christians and non-Christians alike.

Irish travellers

There are about 15000 Irish travellers in the UK. They are a centuries-old ethnic community that travels around in mobile homes. They have their own culture, customs, traditions and language.

The Muslim community

Almost all of the Muslim population in Britain are descendants of the families who came to Britain in the 1950s, 60s and 70s. However, Islam has been followed in Britain for centuries. At least 300 years ago, Indian–Muslim sailors, recruited by the East India Company, settled in port towns. The first mosque in Britain probably opened in Cardiff in 1860. Today, there are Muslim communities all over Britain.

Check your understanding

1 Explain why people can belong to more than one community and why there is an overlap between communities.

2 Describe what each of the communities shown on page 8 has in common. What makes each one a community?

Another point of view

'It is easier to feel part of a community if you live in a village or small town rather than a city.'

Key terms

community: a group of people who are in close contact and who share common interests and values

neighbourhood: a local area within which people live as neighbours, sharing living space and interests

1.2 Where are your roots?

Getting you thinking

Whose genes?

I live in Cheddar in Somerset. My DNA tells me I'm descended from a man who lived here 40 000 years ago.

I live in London and I know my family came from Yorkshire. My DNA tells me I have relatives who were Mongolian, Brazilian, a Russian and a woman who lived near the Mediterranean 117 000 years ago.

I thought I was British but my DNA tells me I'm descended from Native Americans. They must have been brought here.

1 Many of us know where our grandparents lived and perhaps our great grandparents. Where did yours come from?

2 Do you think it is important for you to know your roots? Explain your answer.

3 If we know we have lots of different roots, does it help us to understand others?

'To forget your ancestors is to be a tree without roots.'
Chinese proverb

A pick-and-mix people

Throughout its history, people have settled in Britain from many different countries. They brought their language, ideas and customs, all of which have mixed together to make up the country's culture.

Warlike invasions of Romans, Saxons, Vikings and Normans were followed by peaceful migrations from Europe and many former British colonies. Just look in a dictionary, phone book or at a map to find words and names from many languages.

- In the past 250 years, about six million people have come from Ireland in search of a better life. Many came to the UK during the potato famine of the 1840s.

- In 1860, a quarter of the population of Liverpool were Irish migrants.

- Poles have lived here ever since the reign of Queen Elizabeth I, but the majority of UK Poles settled here after the Second World War when Poland was occupied first by the Nazis and then by the Soviet army.

- There has been a Jewish population in the UK for hundreds of years, but most arrived in the 1930s and 1940s. They came to the UK to escape religious and racial persecution in Russia and Europe.

- In the 1950s, many people from British colonies in Africa, Asia and the Caribbean settled in the UK looking for work, as there was a shortage of manual and semiskilled employees in Britain during this period.

- In the 1970s, thousands of Ugandan Asians arrived here after being expelled from Uganda.

- As more countries have joined the European Union, people from Eastern Europe, including Poland, have come to the UK to work because there are more opportunities.

Immigration today is more restricted for people from many parts of the world.

In the same way that people from other countries come to Britain, people emigrate from Britain to go and live in other countries. The table below shows some reasons for **immigration** and **emigration** in Britain.

Why do people come and go? (thousands)

	Immigration	Emigration	Balance
For work	103.4	92.8	10.6
With a partner	77.2	51.1	26.1
For study	91.2	13.7	77.5
Other	164.6	99.3	65.3
No reason	27.7	49.2	−21.5

Source: Office for National Statistics

You will find out about the diverse communities in the UK and the changes that are taking place.

1.2 Where are your roots?

Ethnic minorities in each region

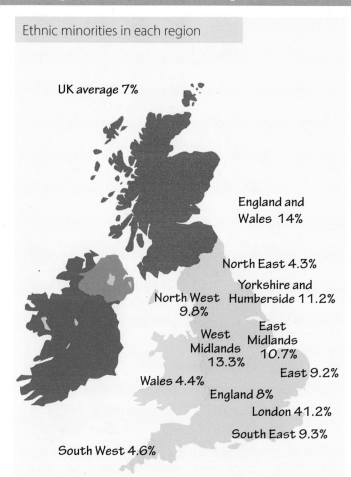

UK average 7%

England and Wales 14%

North East 4.3%

Yorkshire and Humberside 11.2%

North West 9.8%

West Midlands 13.3%

East Midlands 10.7%

East 9.2%

Wales 4.4%

England 8%

London 41.2%

South East 9.3%

South West 4.6%

Source: 2011 Census, Office for National Statistics

Changing patterns in the UK

Ethnic groups 2001 and 2011, England and Wales

		Percentages	
		2001	2011
White		91.3	86.0
Asian/Asian British	Indian	2.0	2.5
	Pakistani	1.4	2.0
	Bangladeshi	0.5	0.8
	Chinese	0.4	0.7
	Other Asian	0.5	1.5
Black/African/ Caribbean/Black British	African	0.9	1.8
	Caribbean	1.1	1.1
	Other Black	0.2	0.5
Mixed ethnic groups		1.4	2.2
Other ethnic group	Arab		0.4
	Any other ethnic group	0.4	0.6

The population of the UK has changed constantly over hundreds of years. Every 10 years, the government carries out a survey of the population to find out about the changes taking place. This is known as the **census**.

A question on people's **ethnic** group was first asked in the 1991 census. It was included to help governments monitor equal opportunities and antidiscrimination policies. It also helps governments to plan for the future.

Action

Research the background and culture of any immigrant groups that have settled in your local area. Find out why they left their homelands, and to what extent they have been able to retain their language and culture. Present your findings to the class.

Another point of view

'People should be free to move where they want.'

Check your understanding

1 Suggest two reasons why the UK is a culturally diverse society.

2 Why did many immigrants come to Britain in the 1950s?

3 In which regions, outside London, would you find the most culturally diverse communities?

4 Do you think other regions of the UK will become more culturally diverse in future? Give reasons.

5 What changes have been taking place to the ethnic mix of the UK?

6 What do you think can be done to bring different ethnic groups together?

Key terms

census: an official count of the population to find out about the changes taking place

emigration: leaving your homeland to live in another country

ethnic: someone's cultural background

immigration: coming to another country to live there

1.3 Religious understanding

Getting you thinking

1 Which symbol represents the religion represented by each building?

2 Think of some other religions that are not shown.

3 What do all these religions have in common? List as many as you can.

Diverse views

Although most UK citizens would probably claim to be Christians, there are many other diverse religious groups in the UK. The majority of these are found in large cities, such as London, Birmingham, Manchester and Leeds, where most of the UK's ethnic **minority** communities live. This religious diversity is the result of people settling here over many years, mostly from former British colonies.

The main ethnic minority groups and their religions are:

- **Bangladeshis:** mostly Muslim (small number of Hindus)

- **Indians (Punjabis):** mostly Sikh, some Hindus

- **Indians (Gujaratis):** mostly Hindus, some Muslims

- **Pakistanis:** Muslim

- **Chinese:** Christian, Confucian and Buddhist

- **Afro-Caribbeans:** Christian and Rastafarian.

Within many religions there are different 'branches'. Anglicans, Methodists, Quakers and Catholics are all part of the wider Christian tradition but practise their religion in different ways. In the same way, Orthodox and Reform Jews share many beliefs but worship in separate synagogues.

Sometimes an individual's clothes, the food they eat or the language they speak gives you a clue to their religion. But this is not always the case.

Changes in religious beliefs in the UK

	2001 (%)	2011 (%)
Christianity	71.6	59.5
Islam	3.0	4.8
Hinduism	1.0	1.3
Sikhism	0.6	0.7
Judaism	0.5	0.4
Buddhism	0.3	0.4
Other religion	0.3	0.4
No religion	14.8	25.1

Source: Office for National Statistics

You will find out about the religious diversity of the UK and why religious tolerance is important.

1.3 Religious understanding

Religion in conflict

Threatened for converting ....

A Bradford man who faced threats and harassment for converting to Christianity from Islam was told by police to 'stop being a crusader and move to another place'.

Nissar Hussain and his wife, Qubra, converted from Islam to Christianity. They were subsequently alienated from family and friends.

As news of the couple's conversion spread, their Bradford home was vandalised and their car was set on fire. Mr Hussain was told that if he did not return to Islam, his house would be burnt down.

I go to an Asian church ....

Another Christian explains: 'I go to church with my family every Sunday. We can wear our Indian clothes and meet other Asian and English friends who we may not see during the week. Going to an Asian church means we worship God in both the English and the Indian traditions.

During the service, one person usually stands up at the front and leads the service. We sing in different languages, including English, as many of the church members are Asian, although people from other nationalities sometimes come along.

We also have Indian instruments to help with the singing and worship. People pray in different languages too. Both men and women pray. In most Asian churches the men and women usually sit on separate sides. The young people sit on both sides, depending on their age, and whether both of their parents come to church.'

1 Why do you think Nissar and Qubra's friends and family disliked them converting?

2 The Asian church is a Christian church. How is it trying to bring people together?

Everyone's right

The United Nations (UN), an international organisation to which most countries belong, put together a Declaration of Human Rights (see page 28). This Declaration includes a section on religion, which states that everyone is free to follow any religion or to choose to follow none. Everyone has the right to join an established religion, or to start a sect or cult of their own. Nobody should be prevented from following the religion of their choice.

Action

Look at the data on this page and do some research to find out how the religious makeup of your area compares with that of the UK as a whole.

Another point of view

'It is always important to be **tolerant** of other people's religious beliefs.'

Check your understanding

1 Why does the UK have such a diversity of religions? Can you name any other countries where you find the same religious diversity?

2 What does the Universal Declaration of Human Rights say about your religious freedom? Is this always observed?

3 What changes in religious belief have taken place in the UK?

Key terms

minority: a small part of a larger group of people

tolerant: open-minded, accepting

Getting you thinking

1 Make a list of the way the government will have to support these children as they grow up and grow old.

2 People are living longer, so what problem does this cause for the government?

Is the population growing?

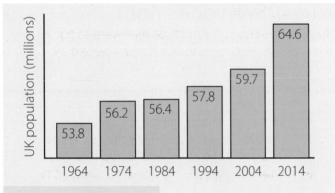

UK population in millions

Source: Office for National Statistics

The UK population has grown steadily throughout history. Many babies used to die at a young age in the early 20th century. Today the survival rate is much higher.

People used to die much earlier than most people do today. This is because most people now have a better diet and better healthcare.

The size of the population has also been affected by world events. The pyramid graph shows the number of males and females in each age group in 2014. A lot of babies were born in the years after the Second World War. These people are now all heading for age 70. You can see that the bars showing 60–69 year olds are longer than you might expect. At the beginning of the 21st century, the number of babies fell, and then rose again more recently. In the bar chart above, you can see the longer lines in recent years, showing more babies being born.

Is the population ageing?

If more babies are being born than the number of people who die, the average age of the population will fall. If it is the other way round, the average age will rise and the population will be ageing. As medical care improves, people are living longer. If the population is ageing, the bars at the top of the pyramid graph will grow longer. One third of people born today can expect to live to 100.

An ageing population generally means that there are more disabled people. The government has to work out how to pay for more pensions, healthcare and looking after the elderly.

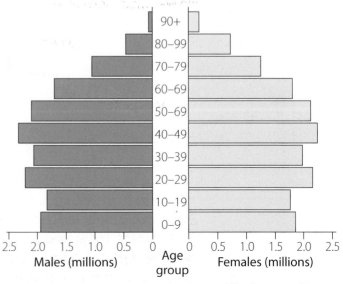

Source: Office for National Statistics

What's causing the change?

Since 1964 the population of the UK has grown by over ten million people. About half of this growth has happened since 2001.

There are two main factors that cause a change in the size of the population.

1 Life expectancy

If people live longer and more babies survive, the population will grow.

2 Migration

The number of immigrants coming into the country and the number of emigrants who go to live in other countries will affect the size of the UK population. As you found out on page 10, there has always been migration into the UK. As the numbers rise and fall, the total number of people in the country will be affected.

Where have the migrants come from?

After the Second World War, the UK was short of people to work in the health service and other jobs. People were encouraged to come from the West Indies and other **Commonwealth** countries to take up these roles.

The second source of immigrants in recent years has been the **European Union** (EU). Member countries of the EU agree that people can move freely from one country to another. As the EU has grown, many people have decided to come to work here.

Why do people want to come to the UK?

People have many reasons for wanting to come to live in the UK. They generally fall into one of the following categories.

- **Economic migrants** come because they are looking for a better life. They want to find work and support themselves and their families.
- **Refugees** come because they have been forced to leave their country in order to escape war, persecution or natural disaster.
- **Asylum seekers** come because they want to put in a request to be allowed to stay here because they are refugees.

Check your understanding

1 What is happening to the size of the UK population?
2 Why is it changing?
3 What effect will the change in age structure have on the country?
4 Since the Second World War, which areas have people come from?
5 What different groups of people want to come to live in the UK?

Action

Look at the following website to track future change in the UK population: http://www.ons.gov.uk/ons/interactive/uk-population-pyramid---dvc1/index.html

Another point of view

'We should welcome everyone who is escaping war, persecution or disaster.'

Key terms

asylum seeker: someone who says he or she is a refugee, but whose claim has not yet been definitively evaluated

Commonwealth: a voluntary group of independent countries, some of which were former British colonies

economic migrant: a person who travels from one country or area to another in order to improve their standard of living

European Union: a group of 28 countries which work together in fields such as the environment, social issues, the economy and trade

refugee: a person who has been forced to leave their country in order to escape war, persecution, or natural disaster

1.5 Migration: the pros and cons

Getting you thinking

What's the economic benefit?

Immigrant workers fill skill gaps and do jobs British workers do not want.

Local economies benefit because migrants can have different skills that could lead to new businesses being set up. They tend to be more **entrepreneurial**. Immigrants also help local businesses because of their links with their home country.

Source: Institute for Public Policy Research

Morrissey said:

"[W]ith the issue of immigration, it's very difficult because although I don't have anything against people from other countries, the higher the influx into England the more the British identity disappears. If you travel to Germany, it's still absolutely Germany. If you travel to Sweden, it still has a Swedish identity. But travel to England and you have no idea where you are... If you walk through Knightsbridge you'll hear every accent apart from an English accent."

1. How can immigrant workers help the economy?
2. What aspects of our culture do you think have changed because of immigration? What has stayed the same?

Immigration – the balance

Immigrants in the UK have given us all sorts of benefits as they have widened our experiences – from food to clothes and entertainment. Many people welcome this **diversity**. They also help the **economy**, as you saw in 'Getting you thinking', but there can also be problems.

People may fear that new arrivals might change their community. They may also feel that new people might threaten their jobs and pay. There is evidence, however, that immigrants take jobs that residents do not want. People from new EU countries may come to pick fruit, for example. They are brought here because farmers can't find enough pickers.

Many people want to come to the UK because they speak English, which makes it easier to get a job.

When the economy is booming, people are welcome because there are more jobs than people. If unemployment starts rising, things may change.

Sometimes immigrants feel that they are left out. The attitude of both immigrants and those who fear their arrival can sometimes cause difficulties as we have seen in cities across the country. There have been some disturbances in cities where ethnic groups are living, but many communities exist happily together.

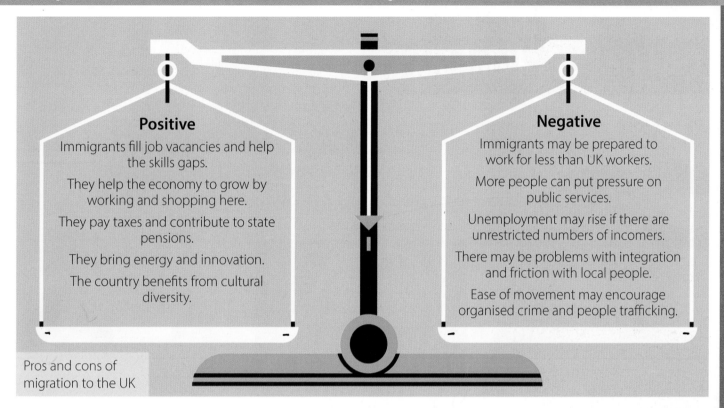

Positive

Immigrants fill job vacancies and help the skills gaps.

They help the economy to grow by working and shopping here.

They pay taxes and contribute to state pensions.

They bring energy and innovation.

The country benefits from cultural diversity.

Negative

Immigrants may be prepared to work for less than UK workers.

More people can put pressure on public services.

Unemployment may rise if there are unrestricted numbers of incomers.

There may be problems with integration and friction with local people.

Ease of movement may encourage organised crime and people trafficking.

Pros and cons of migration to the UK

The challenge

As people from different countries have come to live here, the government has tried to help everyone live together while maintaining their individual identities. You will find out more about how this works on page 26.

Some people feel that **integration** means that ethnic groups will lose their identities. Others feel that it will help them to be more successful members of UK society.

The government wants to control the number of migrants from non-EU countries and the rules are becoming stricter. Immigration today is more restricted for people from many parts of the world.

A points-based scheme has been set up to work out whether an individual can work in the UK. If you are highly skilled, a successful entrepreneur with money to invest, or have been to a UK university, you may be accepted.

Action

Carry out research to compare the ethnic mix in your area with two other places. What differences do you find?

Check your understanding

1 What benefits do immigrants bring to the British economy?

2 What benefits do immigrants bring to British society?

3 Why are some people anxious about immigration?

4 What problems can immigration bring to a country?

Another point of view

'The government must prevent all immigrants coming to the UK.'

Key terms

economy: this is made up of all the organisations that provide goods and services, and all the individuals and organisations that buy them

entrepreneur: a person who sets up a business and takes on financial risks in the hope of making a profit

diversity: the range of different groups that make up a wider population

integration: bringing different groups of people together in society

1.6 What is identity?

Getting you thinking

> I come from Brighton. My parents are divorced. I've got one brother and two half-sisters. I like watching TV and listening to music. I spend loads of time at the beach with my friends.

> I've got Asian roots. I love sport, have loads of mates and I'm always having fun.

> I'm from Newcastle. I'm 15, an only child and a huge fan of *EastEnders* and reality TV shows.

1. What has contributed to the identity of each of these people?

2. How do you think these factors have affected them?

3. How much does your identity depend on where you live, on your family's roots or on your religion?

4. If you had been asked the question 'Who are you?' when you were five years old, what would you have said? How would you answer this question now?

5. Make a list of factors that will shape your identity as you get older.

Who am I?

In some countries, such as France, all citizens must carry an **identity card**. This card gives details such as your name, address and date of birth. But the word '**identity**' has another, broader meaning. The identity of a person is a combination of where they come from and the influences on their life.

Your identity develops and changes as you develop and change. Can you remember how you felt when you first went to school? You've learned a lot about yourself in the 10 or more years since then. You now have a better understanding of your good and bad points; you are more self-aware and aware of how other people see you. Looking back, that five-year-old 'you' will seem like a very different person. Your identity will continue to develop further as you grow older and as you become an employee, a parent, partner/wife/husband and so on. An identity card obviously can't show all this information about you. However, some governments like them because it means that people can be identified easily.

Defining identity

To work out a person's identity, you would need to ask lots of questions. Here are some that might help.

Are you male or female?

Which country and town do you call home?

Do you have any religious belief? If so, which religion do you belong to?

How old are you?

Where were you born?

Which ethnic group do you belong to?

Are both your parents from the same country, region or town?

Where do you live?

Do you belong to social groups with an interest in sport or music, for example?

If you try to answer these questions yourself, you probably find that you have some contradictory answers. Even if you live in England, you might feel Scottish or Welsh. Are you British or European? Perhaps you think of yourself as both. If you are a member of an ethnic minority, you may also feel British or perhaps you feel you have stronger links with the country your family has come from. Anyone who feels they have more than one identity is said to have a **multiple identity**.

In the UK, many people feel they have a multiple identity because of their heritage. Earlier in this section, you discovered that people have come to England from all over the world.

The UK is made up of four nations (England, Scotland, Wales and Northern Ireland), which means that people can have multiple identities. This has led to a debate about how the nations should be governed. As you will find out in Theme B, Wales and Scotland campaigned to have their own governments. Wales now has a National Assembly. Scotland, which has its own parliament, held a vote in a bid for complete independence from the UK. This was narrowly lost.

Check your understanding

1 What does multiple identity mean?
2 Describe how a multiple identity can sometimes lead to conflict.

Another point of view

'People are more alike than different.'

Key terms

identity: who or what someone or something is
identity card: a card that establishes someone's identity
multiple identity: when a person feels they have more than one identity

1.7 Respect and communities

Getting you thinking

Hasaan, a Muslim teenager, suffered daily taunts about his race and religion at school. He was one of only two Asian students at a school where there are 1300 students.

He was called a 'terrorist', told that his mother would be stabbed if she came to school in a headscarf and was asked if he had a bomb in his bag.

After endless torment, he threatened one of the bullies with a knife.

He was taken to court and sentenced to 130 hours of unpaid work.

Since then, he has moved to a school where there has been no abuse. He has now gone to college.

1 Why do you think the students at the school treated Hasaan in this way?

2 What effects do this sort of behaviour have on the school community?

3 Why do you think Hasaan responded as he did?

4 How should schools deal with issues like this?

What is respect?

People have all sorts of definitions of **respect**. Here are a few.

Show consideration for other people's feelings and interests.

Treat people as you would expect to be treated.

Accepting people as they are.

Not putting people down because they're different from you.

An attitude demonstrating that you value another person.

Valuing each other's points of views.

Why is it important to respect other people?

Any community in which people do not have respect for each other will have problems. Whether it is a school, workplace or club, a lack of respect will cause friction and may result in the law being broken. You will find out more about how the law protects people later in this Theme.

Respect and human rights

The need for respect has been long established but not always acted upon. The **United Nations** wrote the Universal Declaration of Human Rights in 1948 to set out the basic rights for all individuals. All the expectations of respect are included in the declaration. It underpins the way individuals should be treated by each other, governments and all other organisations. You will find out more on page 28.

Action

Look at the Universal Declaration of Human Rights.
http://www.un.org/en/documents/udhr/

Which 'articles' support treating people with respect?

Making respect work

The University of Essex is a diverse community where everyone is expected to treat each other with dignity and respect.

It asks students and anyone working at the university to agree to the following principles.

All members of the University community:

- are to be treated fairly and given equality of opportunity, free from all forms of **discrimination**, **harassment** and **victimisation**
- have the right to live their life in their own way, as long as their actions do not negatively affect others
- have the right to live in a secure and welcoming environment free from negative behaviour
- have the right to use shared spaces to work without disturbance or unnecessary distraction.

By committing to these principles, I will:

- be considerate of those around me and treat others as I would like to be treated
- treat others with dignity and respect
- take care of my community and environment for the benefit of all who live, work, study and visit here
- take responsibility for those that I invite into our community
- positively contribute to my community through my behaviour.

1 Why do you think the University of Essex has a respect agreement with students and staff?

2 What rights do members of the university community have?

3 What is expected on students and staff?

4 How do you think this agreement helps life at the university?

5 In your own words – how would you explain respect?

Another point of view

'We don't need to have respect. People should just stick up for themselves.'

Check your understanding

1 Use the statements in bubbles on page 20 to come up with your own definition of respect.

2 What problems occur when people do not respect each other?

3 How are people protected if lack of respect becomes a serious issue?

4 Why is it necessary for large organisations to have polices about respect?

Key terms

discrimination: treating someone less favourably because of their colour, ethnic origins, age, gender or disability

harassment: repeatedly threatening, humiliating or pestering someone

respect: show consideration for someone's feelings, wishes or rights

United Nations: an international organisation that tries to encourage peace, cooperation and friendship between countries

victimisation: discriminating against someone unfairly

1.8 Meeting barriers

Getting you thinking

Some children were playing on the beach when an old 'bag lady' came along. She was talking to herself and picking things up off the beach as she walked. Parents called their children over and told them to stay close by, until the old woman had moved on. The following day, they discovered that the old woman came to the beach every day, picking up bits of glass so children wouldn't cut their feet.

1 Why did the parents call their children over? What is the moral of the story?

2 Have you ever misjudged somebody because of their dress or behaviour? Have you ever been misjudged?

3 Think of individuals or groups who are misjudged in this way, and say why they have been misunderstood.

Prejudice and discrimination

People treat each other badly for all sorts of reasons. Such unfair treatment can mean that people don't get jobs or are kept out of clubs, as well as many other things. The case studies that follow show some strategies used to overcome prejudice and discrimination. Think about how discrimination is affecting each person.

The pyramid of discrimination

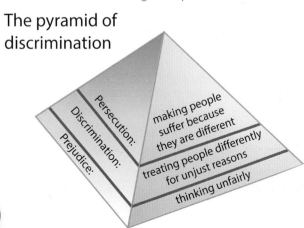

Persecution: making people suffer because they are different

Discrimination: treating people differently for unjust reasons

Prejudice: thinking unfairly

Part of the 'rough and tumble' of school? ....

Lancaster Youth and Community Service set up a group for gay and lesbian young people, to help them cope with the **homophobic** bullying they encountered in schools and colleges. One young man who belongs to the group said, 'I love coming here. It's the only time in the week I feel completely safe. It's the one place I can be myself.'

1 What does the young man's comment tell you about homophobic bullying?

2 What can schools do to reduce homophobic bullying?

You will find out about discrimination and consider how it affects people and how it might be overcome.

'Education is the answer' . . . .

Although there are many black and Asian football players and they are accepted by football fans everywhere, there are still problems with racial prejudice and discrimination. Some fans have been known to call out racist comments and make monkey noises when black players are on the pitch.

Sir Alex Ferguson, who was Manchester United's manager, is a supporter of football's equality and inclusion organisation Kick It Out. This is what he says:

'I think it's all down to education and how people are brought up. I was brought up in a family where there was never any prejudice. I think education from family and school is the most important thing. If parents are saying to their kids, 'Don't play with that Charlie down the road because he is black,' what message does that give? I think education is the secret.'

The situation today is better than it was 20 years ago, and 20 years ago it was better than 30 years ago. So progress eventually eliminates a lot of what is going on.

1   Do you agree with Sir Alex that 'it's all down to education'? Give reasons.

2   Why do you think things are improving?

3   Why do you think all top clubs and star football players in the UK support the Kick It Out campaign?

Another point of view

'Discrimination is the result of ignorance.'

Action

Use the Kick It Out website, www.kickitout.org, to research what your local football clubs, professional and amateur, are doing to combat **racism**.

Young and Powerful . . . .

Young and Powerful is a group of young disabled and non disabled people supported by Comic Relief. They all go to mainstream schools and campaign for **inclusive education**. They believe all children need to be taught together, so they can learn from each other.

1   What does the phrase 'inclusive education' mean?

2   What kinds of physical barriers would a wheelchair-user face if they came to your school? Would they face any other kinds of barriers?

Check your understanding

1   What is prejudice? Why are some people prejudiced against others?

2   What is discrimination? Give some examples.

3   Look at the different cases on these two pages and say whether the people or groups described could have experienced prejudice, discrimination or persecution.

4   How are the people in each story overcoming prejudice?

5   How does discrimination affect people's lives?

Key terms

homophobic: fearing or hating gay or bisexual people

inclusive education: schooling that involves everyone, regardless of disability or non disability

racism: the idea that some people of different origins are not as good as others

23

1.9 Discrimination and the law

Getting you thinking

WHO SAYS ETHNIC MINORITIES CAN'T GET JOBS? THERE ARE OPENINGS EVERYWHERE.

Lavatory attendant. Office cleaner. Somebody has to do all the low-paid, menial jobs, but why is it so often people from ethnic minorities? Prejudice, racial discrimination and harassment are denying people the choice of job they deserve. It's unjust and unfair. More than that, it's a terrible waste of British talent.

1 What message is the poster giving?

2 What other forms of discrimination take place at work?

3 Why do people need protection against discrimination?

4 How do you think the law can help?

Fighting discrimination with the law

Everyone deserves a fair chance to be successful in life. Poster campaigns and other public awareness programmes try to educate people to think beyond prejudice. These campaigns are just one way of dealing with **discrimination**. There are also legal ways of tackling prejudice and discrimination.

The Equality Act

The Equality Act 2010 is the law which bans unfair treatment and helps achieve equal opportunities in the workplace and in wider society. It replaced previous anti-discrimination laws with a single Act to make the law simpler. It also strengthened protection in some situations.

There are nine protected characteristics which cannot be used as a reason to treat people unfairly. Every person has one or more of the protected characteristics, so the Act protects everyone against unfair treatment. The protected characteristics are:

- age
- disability
- gender reassignment
- marriage and civil partnership
- pregnancy and maternity
- race
- religion or belief
- sex
- sexual orientation.

How has the law helped?

Look at these cases where the anti-discrimination Act has helped people.

Maintenance manager wins sex discrimination case

Laetitia Booth had been a maintenance manager on the railways. When the company was reorganised she was given a lower-status job. She sued the company for sex discrimination and unfair dismissal and won.

1 Do you think that maintenance managers on the railways are mainly men or women?

2 Do you think this had any effect on the company's decision?

3 How did the law protect her?

Deaf man wins damages

Keith Wynn is profoundly deaf. He applied for a job with Multipulse Electronics Ltd. He was well qualified as he had held a similar job in another company for 25 years. Multipulse cancelled his interview because they had not organised a sign language interpreter. He heard nothing more. He challenged them in court and won considerable damages.

1 What did Multipulse Electronics do wrong?

2 How did the law protect Mr Wynn?

£2.8 million **compensation** for suffering racial discrimination

Balbinder Chagger from Hayes, Middlesex, worked as a £100 000-a-year trading risk controller for a bank until he was made redundant. He claimed that he lost his job because of racial discrimination. A woman with a similar performance history got the job.

The court heard that Chagger would never find equivalent work again and should be compensated on the basis that he would lose 75 per cent of earnings for the rest of his working life. The bank planned to appeal.

1 Why did Mr Chagger think he should have had the job?

2 How does the law protect people from racial discrimination?

3 Why do you think the bank planned to appeal against the amount of damages?

4 How does the law protect people from racial discrimination?

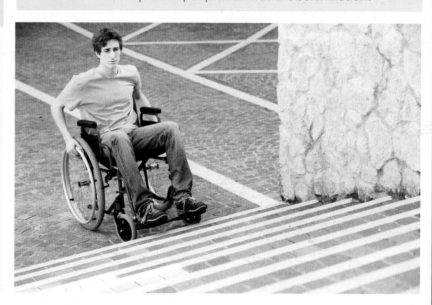

Action

What does your school do to ensure equal opportunities for all students and staff?

Contact Scope or look on their website (www.scope.org.uk) to find out about their Schools Access Initiative.

Check your understanding

1 Which groups of people are protected by the Equality Act?

2 What is the connection between respect and these legal rights?

Another point of view

'Public awareness campaigns are enough to deal with the problem of discrimination.'

Key terms

compensation: making amends for something; something given to make good a loss

discrimination: treating someone less favourably because of their colour, ethnic origins, gender or disability

Getting you thinking

Supporting new communities

Fenland in Eastern England has a changing population. New communities are settling here bringing both advantages and new challenges around cohesion and **integration**.

To reduce tensions and misunderstandings, Fenland District Council has set up:

- community advice and guidance sessions – helping over 500 people per month access advice, information and services
- Community Mediators – helping to resolve misunderstandings in and between the settled and Eastern European communities
- learning English – enabling people from an Eastern European background to learn basic English
- training for people who have learned English to become community translators
- Migrant Population Advisors – helping Eastern European families to access Council services
- New Arrivals Welcome Pack – to help people understand the laws and traditions of the local area
- community events celebrating our diverse communities, including food tasting and festivals.

Oldham Youth Council

What do we do?
We work with loads of different services and organisations to make sure that young people are able to shape and influence decisions that affect our lives.

We aim to…
Promote and encourage activities, events and opportunities for young people and encourage communication between young people and local and national government.

Raise the profile of young people in a positive way.

Represent Oldham young people in national and regional initiatives, such as the British Youth Council and the United Kingdom Youth Parliament.

Work on projects and campaigns that address a range of issues that affect young people.

Ensure that we are aware of the needs of young people who experience disadvantage or are unable to speak for themselves.

You will discover how schools and communities can be inclusive and promote community cohesion.

1.10 Developing mutual understanding

International Week at Berger School

International week has been running for more than 10 years at Berger School in Hackney, East London. It is an opportunity for pupils and parents to share our vast diversity and rich cultures.

This year we will celebrate the United Kingdom, which is a first for us. We will also be celebrating the Caribbean, Asia, Africa and South America through various dance, drumming and storytelling workshops in the classroom. The whole school will also take part in a carnival parade, with parents invited to join us to bring this fascinating week to an end! A special menu will be provided for the children to try new delicious cultural food each day.

1 How are these three organisations working in diverse communities?

2 How do they encourage community cohesion?

3 How successful do you think they will be?

What is a diverse community?

A diverse community is made up of people with a range of identities. They may be different because of their gender, ethnicity, religion, age, disability or social class. Across the UK there are many examples of diverse communities. Many cities have a mix of people from different ethnic and religious groups. Most places have people from different age groups, but some have a concentration of older people. This is often true of seaside resorts because retired people want to live by the sea.

Making diverse communities work

In most places, people with different identities get along happily, but sometimes tensions flare up. There have been examples of disturbances and even riots in ethnically diverse communities.

Schools, local government and other organisations are expected by the government to help **community cohesion**. They all have statements of the way they encourage community cohesion. In 'Getting you thinking', you have seen some ways different organisations make their communities work.

Why is community cohesion important?

If everyone is to play their part in society, they need to live together happily. If there is friction, people often will not want to join in. if communities are integrated, people are more likely to participate.

To become a UK citizen, people must learn some English and take a test which shows that they have some understanding of the country's history, how **democracy** works and the features of everyday life. This helps them to feel part of the community and they will be more likely to participate in the UK's democratic society. You will find out more about democracy in Theme B.

Action

What does your school do to contribute to community cohesion?

Another point of view

'If people's differences are ignored, they will all get on in the end.'

Check your understanding

1 What is community cohesion?

2 How can different organisations support community cohesion?

3 Why is community cohesion important?

4 Why are people who are integrated more likely to participate in society?

Key terms

community cohesion: creating a community where there is a sense of belonging for all communities and people's different backgrounds are valued

democracy: government by the people, either directly or through elected representatives

integration: bringing different groups of people together in society

Getting you thinking

1 What are these children deprived of?

2 Make a list of the things you think every child should have.

3 Use your list to write a statement of children's rights.

Human rights

People all over the world suffer because their basic needs are not met. Some people's freedoms are limited by the country in which they live. Nobody should live without these basic **human rights:**

- the right to education
- the right to work
- the right to fair conditions at work
- the right to travel
- the right to food and clothes
- the right to healthcare
- the right to meet with friends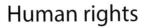
- the right to own property
- the right to follow your religion
- the right to marry and have children
- the rights of minorities to be treated the same as the majority.

1 Which of the rights listed above are the most important to you? Why?

2 Can you think of some situations where any of your rights might be threatened?

3 What examples are there in the news of people's human rights being threatened?

The United Nations and human rights

The **United Nations** is an international organisation. It was set up in 1945 and most countries in the world now belong to it. Together, these members have developed two important statements of human rights. The Universal Declaration of Human Rights was created in 1948 and the Convention on the Rights of the Child was agreed in 1989.

They set out moral standards for everyone, everywhere; but in many parts of the world people's human rights are still abused. The **Declaration** offers guidance for countries but cannot be enforced legally if a country's laws do not take it up.

The Convention on the Rights of the Child (CRC) . . . .

This **Convention** requires governments all around the world to think about the needs of young people and to consult them about matters that affect them, such as education, family life, law and order. Millions of young people do not have relatives to look after them: those caught up in civil wars in Africa, for instance. The CRC recognises this and says that young people must have rights of their own – rights that don't depend on parents or other adults.

There are still 250 000 children serving as soldiers around the world. The CRC states that 'Governments should not allow children under 15 to join the army.'

Universal Declaration of Human Rights (UDHR) . . . .

The UDHR was drawn up by world leaders after the Second World War. They wanted to prevent such terrible things happening again. It states that everyone has a right to life and liberty, freedom of speech and movement, a fair wage, a fair trial, education , privacy, opinion and association, tolerance and respect, equality and representation, and other human rights.

Huang Qi was arrested. He had been involved in assisting families to bring a legal case against the local authorities. Their children had died when school buildings collapsed in an earthquake.

Action

Collect newspaper reports and internet articles concerned with human rights. Discuss the effects that being deprived of these rights can have on people.

Another point of view

'People should learn to look after themselves rather than being protected by declarations and conventions.'

Check your understanding

1 Why was the Universal Declaration of Human Rights written?

2 Does everyone have the rights that are set out in these statements of rights? Give examples.

Key terms

convention: an agreement (often between governments)
declaration: a document setting down aims and intentions
human rights: things that people are morally or legally allowed to do or have
United Nations: an international organisation that tries to encourage peace, cooperation and friendship between countries

Getting you thinking

Right to free elections

'Free elections will be held at reasonable intervals by secret ballot, under conditions which will ensure the free expression of the opinion of the people in the choice of the legislature.'

Article 3 European Convention on Human Rights

This section of the European Convention on Human Rights means that everyone should be able to vote, even if they are in prison. British Law excludes prisoners.

A group of people in prison took the UK government to the European Court of Human Rights, complaining that they were not allowed to vote. They won and the UK government was told it had to change the law. This would bring it into line with most other European countries.

1 Set out arguments for why prisoners should – and should not – have the vote.

2 If you were in prison, how would you feel about not being able to vote?

3 What effect would having a vote have on your view of your place in society?

Magna Carta: the start of rights in the UK

In 1215, King John had to make peace with the barons. His reign had been corrupt and violent. The barons demanded that King John stopped taxing them heavily and persecuting the citizens.

Magna Carta, or the Great Charter, was signed by King John and the barons. The King promised many things, but the most important today is this statement:

'No free man shall be seized or imprisoned, or stripped of his rights or possessions, or outlawed or exiled, or deprived of his standing in any other way, nor will we proceed with force against him, or send others to do so, except by the lawful judgment of his equals or by the law of the land. To no-one will we sell, to no-one deny or delay right or justice.'

It really means that everyone is equal before the law and none can be imprisoned without a fair trial. The signing of Magna Carta was also the beginning of Parliament, as it gave powers to the barons and the King could not make decisions on his own.

Magna Carta has influenced the American Bill of Rights, which was written in 1791, and the UN's Universal Declaration of Human Rights, written in 1948.

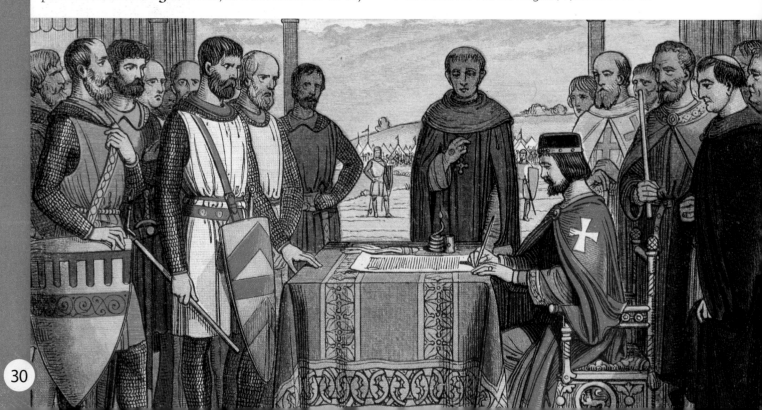

The development of human rights in Europe

After the UN created the Universal Declaration of Human Rights, the countries of Europe adopted it and developed systems to enforce it. The UK has more recently included it in our laws through the Human Rights Act. This means that the UN Declaration has become part of the legal rights of people who live in the UK.

1950 The European Convention on Human Rights (ECHR) ....

This sets the framework for European countries. If the residents of one country don't think they have had a fair response from the courts, they can take their case to the European Court of Human Rights.

1998 Human Rights Act (UK) ....

Since 2000, the UK has had its own laws on human rights, which say that all organisations have a duty to protect the rights of all individuals. These are the rights which are set out in the ECHR. The Human Rights Act protects everyone in the UK.

What's happening to human rights in the UK?

In 'Getting you thinking' you learned about a case in which people are challenging British law by going to the European Court of Human Rights. The European Convention on Human Rights says that everyone can vote – even if they are in prison. UK law prevents this and may have to change

Some people in the UK would like to see The Human Rights Act replaced with a British Bill of Rights and Responsibilities. This could mean that politicians could decide which rights we are entitled to.

European Court of Human Rights

Action
Put the statement from Magna Carta on the page opposite into your own words.

Another point of view
'We should be able to decide which human rights we want to include in British law.'

Check your understanding

1 Explain how Magna Carta has influenced our rights in the UK.

2 In which document are human rights set out in Europe?

3 What is the name of the law that puts these rights into effect in the UK?

4 Why would some people like to see the law in the UK changed?

Key terms
Magna Carta: a charter of rights which the English barons forced King John to sign in 1215

Getting you thinking

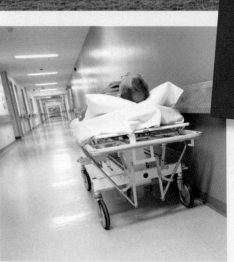

1 What issues do each of these images represent?

2 Do you think we can influence any of these issues?

3 Explain how we can do so.

You can make a difference!

In the UK we have **political rights**. This means that people can have their say and make a real difference. Just as the United Nations has set down everyone's human rights, it has done the same for political rights. We are all entitled:

> to vote and to be elected at genuine elections which shall be held by secret ballot.
>
> *International Covenant of Political Rights*

This means that we live in a democracy in which almost everyone over the age of 18 can **vote** and can also stand as a candidate in an **election**.

Who can we vote for?

- **Locally**
  Whether you live in a town or a rural community, you can vote for people to represent your area. These people are known as councillors and are your first source of help if you are concerned about a local issue.

- **Nationally**
  Every part of the country is represented by a **Member of Parliament**. Most people decide to vote for a candidate who has views they agree with.

- **Internationally**
  The European Union has a parliament, which represents all members of the European Union. We elect **Members of the European Parliament** to have a say in the plans that are developed for Europe.

You will learn more about these organisations, voting and elections later in the course.

You will find out about how your rights have an effect on the way the country is run.

A group of young people in Aldbourne got together to campaign for a BMX track in their village. After raising funds and representing their views at the Parish Council, they achieved their objective – and won the Philip Lawrence award for Good Citizenship. This was just the beginning of their activities. They have become an official Youth Council, which is elected by the young people in the area.

The UN and political rights

Article 21 of the UN Declaration of Human Rights says, 'Everyone has the right to take part in the government of his country, directly or through a freely chosen representative.'

Freedom of speech ....

In the UK we are free to say what we like as long as we don't break the law by discriminating against others or inciting violence. There is even a special place in London where people go to express their views.

People can also organise campaigns and meet to protest against activity they don't like. Without these freedoms, our political rights would be meaningless because it would be very difficult to oppose the government or protest against the activities of other organisations.

Check your understanding

1 What is meant by political rights?

2 How can we use our political rights?

3 How would the UK be different without these rights?

4 What cause have people protested for or against recently?

5 Why are freedom of speech and the freedom to campaign important if people are to put rights into practice?

Another point of view

'We don't need political rights. The government can decide what happens to us.'

Key terms

councillor: a member of a local council, elected by people in the area

election: selection of one or more people for an official position by voting

Member of Parliament: a person who has been elected to represent a part of the country in Parliament

Member of the European Parliament: a person who has been elected to represent a part of the country in the European Parliament

political rights: rights to take part in elections and other democratic activities

vote: to choose a candidate in an election

1.14 Legal rights

Getting you thinking

1 What do these photographs tell you about human rights in the USA in the mid-1900s?

2 Which basic human rights were being denied?

3 Do you think you would see sights like these in the USA today? Give reasons.

What are legal rights?

When law protects a human right, it becomes a **legal right**. For example, everyone has the right to go to public places such as parks, hotels and restaurants. The law changed to make it illegal for anyone to be refused entry to any public place because of his or her ethnicity.

The protection of many of these rights has been brought together in The Equality **Act**, which you found out about on page 24. It protects people from all sorts of discrimination.

The Universal Declaration of Human Rights says you have a right to a fair wage. The Minimum Wage Act made this a legal right, so all adult workers in England and Wales must be paid the minimum wage. The Universal Declaration of Human Rights also says you have a right to 'equal pay for equal work'. The Equality Act made equal pay a legal right.

Turning human rights into legal rights

The right to education

The right to work

The right to meet friends

The right to travel

The right to healthcare

The right to fair conditions at work

The right to vote

The right to food and clothes

The right to follow your religion

The right to own property

The right to life

The right to marry and have children

The rights of minorities to be treated the same as the majority

The right to freedom

The right to privacy

The right to fair trial

The right not to be tortured or punished cruelly

1 Can these human rights all be turned into legal rights? Give reasons.

2 Suggest what these laws might say.

Find out more about legal rights

Human rights and legal rights are a theme throughout this book. You have already explored religious rights and the laws that protect them. The Equality Act helps to protect minorities (page 27). Later in the course, you will find out about laws to protect you at work (page 37) and how your privacy is protected (page 42).

Action

Research recent cases in which the Equality Act has been broken. Which human rights had been ignored in each case?

Another point of view

'Legal rights just protect people from themselves.'

Check your understanding

1 What is the difference between a human right and a legal right?

2 Name one law that makes a human right a legal right.

Key terms

Act: a law passed by Parliament
legal right: a right that is protected by law

Getting you thinking

1 What sorts of problems do you think people might face when at work?

2 How do you think an employer might make their staff's working life better?

3 What effect do you think a happy workforce has on a business?

4 What do you think the law should have to say about working conditions?

Conflict at work

There are many reasons for conflict at work. People may

- be expected to work long hours
- have to work in dangerous and unhealthy working conditions
- receive poor pay
- be dismissed without reason
- not be treated as individuals with individual needs.

Before laws were introduced to protect people, some employers treated their staff unfairly. Employment laws exist to protect the rights of employees and make sure businesses carry out their responsibilities towards their staff. Without these laws, people's human right to fair conditions at work could be harder to protect. Without these laws, there is more likely to be conflict.

Unions

Employees began to form **trade unions** so that they could negotiate with employers to reach fairer agreements on pay and working conditions. Over the years, these agreements have led to huge improvements in the rights of employees.

By trying to persuade employers and Parliament to adopt fairer and safer working practices, the unions proved to be effective pressure groups in looking after the interests of their members. A group of people bargaining together is more powerful than individuals working alone.

Rights in the workplace

The **National Minimum Wage** sets down the minimum anyone can be paid. The **National Living Wage** is a higher amount to be paid to people over 25.

The **Equality Act** protects people from discrimination on many grounds.

The **contract of employment** is an agreement between employer and employee setting out pay and conditions.

Health and safety laws say that employers must provide a safe working environment and train employees to work safely.

What's in a contract? . . . .

- Names of employer and employee
- Entitlement to sick pay
- Date of starting
- Pension details
- Rate of pay and working hours
- Complaints and disciplinary procedures
- Place of work
- Conditions for ending the employment contract
- Holiday entitlement

Check your understanding

1 What human rights can be affected if people are not treated well at work?

2 What areas do the main employment laws cover?

3 What is the contract of employment for?

4 What does a contract of employment cover?

Action

Check your local media for evidence of conflict at work. Was there any resolution? What was the issue? Who won? Why?

Another point of view

'Rights at work are more important than responsibilities.'

Key terms

contract of employment: a document that details an employee's and employer's responsibilities for a particular job

National Living Wage: the minimum amount to be paid to an employee over the age of 25

National Minimum Wage: the minimum amount to be paid to an employee

trade unions: organisations that look after the interests of a group of employees

Getting you thinking

1 Match these questions to the situations. Can I get my money back? Can I get compensation? Can that be true?

2 Who do you think is at fault in each of the examples: the retailer, manufacturer or **consumer**? Explain why.

3 Have you ever had to complain about something you have bought? How did you go about it? What was the result?

The Consumer Rights Act 2015

This law provides you as a consumer with the right to:

- clear and honest information before you buy
- get what you pay for
- goods and digital content that are fit for purpose
- services that are performed with reasonable care and skill
- faults to be put right free of charge or a refund or replacement provided
- a fair contract.

It also affects organisations that enforce the law.

- They can give written notice of routine inspections.
- They can fight for compensation when customers have suffered harm.

If a dispute cannot be resolved informally, you can opt for Alternative Dispute Resolution. This is a process which tries to sort out disputes between a consumer and business, outside the court system. It is therefore quicker and cheaper.

Mediation is usually the first step. It tries to sort out the problem by asking the two sides to set out the case. The mediator will then suggest a solution. If this doesn't work, it will go to an adjudicator or arbitrator who will make decisions that the consumer and business have to accept.

How can you enforce your rights?

If you have bought goods or services and you are dissatisfied with them, you have a right to claim your money back, to make an exchange or to have a repeat of the service.

1 Contact the trader with details of your complaint, say what you want done and give them a chance to put the matter right.

2 If you are not happy with the outcome, you can seek advice from the **Citizens Advice Bureau (CAB)**. They can help with a wide variety of problems, including shopping complaints.

3 The Citizens Advice Bureau may recommend that you go to a **Trading Standards Department**. They can investigate complaints about misleading descriptions or prices, and the safety of consumer goods. They can take action against people who break the law.

4 The **Office of Fair Trading**, a government office, can also take action against traders who break consumer laws.

Sellers have rights too

In certain situations consumers cannot claim refunds or demand exchanges. If you bought a shirt in a sale and you knew it had a defect, you would not be able to claim your money back, because the seller didn't hide the problem from you when you bought it.

Sellers do not have to exchange goods, but most will do so as long as they have not been used. So, if you have bought some clothes and you change your mind about them later, you will find most shops are happy to exchange them, even though they don't have to by law.

Home shopping and the internet

When you buy over the internet from a company trading in the UK, you are covered by more or less the same legislation as that which covers shop purchases:

- the goods you've bought should be of satisfactory quality
- they should be fit for the purpose they are sold for
- they should be as described by the seller.

Action

Working in pairs, think about why traders and businesses prefer to sort out complaints themselves.

Another point of view

'Consumers should look after themselves.'

Check your understanding

1 If you bought a CD at a reduced price because the CD cover was damaged, would you be able to take it back to the shop and claim a refund? Give reasons for your answer.

2 If you bought something from a shop and it was faulty, but the shop refused to refund your money, what could you do?

3 What extra rights do you have when home shopping or shopping over the internet, compared with when you buy something from a shop?

Key terms

Citizens Advice Bureau (CAB): an organisation that offers free advice on consumer and other legal matters

consumer: a person who buys goods or services for their own use

Office of Fair Trading: a government office that can take action against traders who break the law

Trading Standards Department: an official body that enforces consumer-based law

Getting you thinking

Many people are hurt by fireworks each year. Some are seriously hurt.

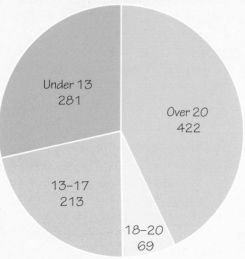

Firework injuries in the UK

Age groups of people injured

- Under 13 — 281
- Over 20 — 422
- 13–17 — 213
- 18–20 — 69

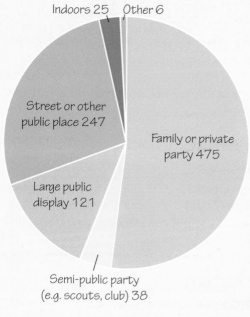

Place where accident occurred

- Indoors 25
- Other 6
- Street or other public place 247
- Family or private party 475
- Large public display 121
- Semi-public party (e.g. scouts, club) 38

Source: Firework injury statistics, BERR

1 You must be over 18 to buy fireworks, and yet over 50 per cent of all injuries were to children under 18. Who do you think is to blame for these accidents:
   - companies that make fireworks
   - shops that sell fireworks
   - parents
   - people who organise public displays
   - the police
   - the children themselves?

   Give reasons for your answer.

2 What would you do to reduce the number of accidents with fireworks?

3 Turn your suggestions for question 2 into a firework safety code.

Rights and responsibilities

Everyone over 18 has a right to buy fireworks. This right, like many others, brings with it certain responsibilities. You must follow the firework code: never throw a lighted firework at anyone, and never set them off in the street, where they might disturb elderly neighbours who have a right to peace and quiet, or alarm pets. If you don't respect the firework code you will not be respecting other people's rights and freedoms.

Rights and responsibilities are best thought of as two sides of the same coin. You have a right to own a bike and ride it down your street, but you also have a **responsibility** to ride it carefully so you don't endanger pedestrians or other road users. For example, if you ride without lights in the dark, not only will you be breaking the law but you could cause a motorist to swerve and crash while trying to avoid you. Even if no one is hurt in the accident, there could be financial consequences for the driver if they need their car to do their job.

You will find out about the need to respect other people's rights and freedoms.

1.17 Rights with responsibilities

All children also have a right to an education, as expressed in the Convention of the Rights of the Child (CRC), but students have a responsibility not to disrupt lessons so others can't learn. You have a right to be respected, but you must also respect others. For example, you have the right to follow a particular religion and would expect your religious views to be respected. In the same way, you must respect the religious views of others.

Moral rights

Many of our rights are laid down in law, but there are others that affect the way in which we behave. There are lots of laws about where people cannot smoke, but they do not say anything about what we do at home. Smoking round small children can affect their health, so parents have a moral responsibility not to do so. The children have a **moral right** to live in a smoke-free environment.

Keeping the law

Not only should people respect others' rights, they should also respect the law.

If people do not keep the law, society will not function well. In some countries people ignore laws when driving, which makes the roads very dangerous. Sometimes people question the law because they don't approve of what is happening – but they may find themselves in court.

The rule of law and democracy

The rule of law means that no one is above the law – even the law makers. Democracy requires everyone to take part in decision making, either directly or through elected representatives. If people don't take their role in democracy seriously, it won't work. If few people vote, for example, it means that the government is selected by a small group of people rather than by the whole electorate. If you don't vote, you can't have your say. If law makers think the law does not apply to them, democracy cannot work effectively. In some parts of the world, the rule of law is ignored by the law makers.

Democratic values

The values of freedom, equality and justice, which you have seen developed through this Theme, aim to create an orderly society in which freedom is preserved. You will find out more about how these values work together in Themes B and C.

Action

Discuss why people in less economically developed countries (LEDCs) do not have their basic needs satisfied. How are their human rights affected?

Another point of view

'People should never have rights without responsibilities.'

Check your understanding

1 List some responsibilities that go with the following rights:
   - the right to an education
   - the right to drink alcohol
   - the right to own and drive a car.
2 What is a moral right?
3 Make a list of as many moral rights as you can.

Key terms

moral right: the responsibility of people to behave in a moral way towards others
responsibility: something it is your duty to do or to look after

Getting you thinking

Freedom of speech . . . .

Everyone has the right to freedom of opinion and expression; this right includes freedom to hold opinions without interference and to seek, receive and give information and ideas through any media and regardless of frontiers.

Privacy . . . .

No one shall be subjected to interference with his privacy, family, home or correspondence, nor to attacks upon his honour and reputation. Everyone has the right to the protection of the law against such interference or attacks.

Is privacy important? . . . .

Jean Bernard Fernandez-Versini, the husband of pop star Cheryl Cole, has won damages from *Heat*. The magazine had published a story about their marriage and family life. He has deliberately chosen not to court the media and has actively sought to avoid publicity for himself and his family.

He has accepted an apology and damages from the publisher of *Heat*.

Is freedom of speech important? . . . .

- A boy drew bombs and said he wanted to be a suicide bomber when he grew up.
- A girl brought **propaganda** leaflets into school to give to the class.
- A boy came to school with a swastika cut into his hair.
- I wouldn't ask a person for the time or directions as I am afraid that they'd call me a terrorist.

Pop star Cheryl Cole and her second husband Jean Bernard Fernandez-Versini

1 Write out the statements about the freedom of speech and privacy in your own words.

2 What are your views on each of the examples about freedom of speech?

3 How does this apply to Jean Bernard Fernandez-Versini?

Why should human rights be limited?

Human rights are generally thought to help people live a just and fair life. They tell us that people should not be treated badly or prevented from doing the things that everyone regards as a normal part of a decent life.

However, there are some occasions when these freedoms may be limited for everyone else's good. You found out about the Equality Act on page 24. This limits people's freedoms in order to protect others from various sorts of discrimination.

There are also laws about slander and libel, which prevent people from saying things that are not true about others. You will find out more about this in Theme D on page 132. Famous people often don't want stories and pictures in the media. Sometimes it is argued that they seek publicity, so they should accept the stories that are printed about them. Prince William has asked to privacy for his children when they are playing in the park. Is this different – because they don't seek publicity?

The threat of terrorism

All our lives have been changed by the threat of terrorism. A holiday abroad, for example, means careful checks of both us and our baggage. There are more serious challenges to human rights in the government's plans to prevent terrorism.

- People can be detained without knowing why – and without a trial.

- People can be prevented from making statements that are inflammatory but do not threaten violence.

- Schools, universities and other public bodies are expected to report people who they think might be a threat.

Governments are always under pressure to keep us safe. Such strategies will inevitably affect our human rights.

Sometimes it may be wise to limit people's human rights, but it is important to strike a fair balance between the competing interests of the individual and of the community as a whole.

Reasons for limiting human rights

- The protection of the reputation or rights of others
- The interests of national security
- The interests of public safety
- Preventing the disclosure of information received in confidence
- The protection of health or morals
- The economic wellbeing of the country
- Maintaining the authority and impartiality of the justice system
- The protection of the rights and freedoms of others
- The prevention of disorder or crime

Action

Find out about any other examples of people challenging the media when they think their privacy has been invaded.

Another point of view

'Human rights should never be limited.'

Check your understanding

1 What is meant by freedom of speech?

2 How can people be offended by things said by other people?

3 How has the threat of terrorism limited our freedoms?

4 Why should our freedoms be limited?

Key terms

propaganda: information, which might be biased or misleading, used to promote a political cause or point of view

Getting you thinking

Can do! 1

The public loos had been a mess for years. There were always people hanging out nearby and vandalising them. No one wanted to use them! Steve, Emma and Akari decided to work out what could be done. They got a group of friends together to think about it.

The local community could do with a loo, but it would have to be indestructible. There would be plenty of space left in the building once modern, new facilities had been installed. All the local kids complained there was nothing to do in the evening. Many sat at home and watched the telly or played computer games – but they never had the latest ones. So they came up with the idea of setting up an internet café in the rest of the space. It could be used by all sorts of people who didn't have a computer or wanted to learn – and it would be a good place to get together.

It would take some work and they'd have to persuade people that it could be done – and they'd need some help.

The local councillor had been into school recently to judge a Citizenship competition. While she was there, she'd explained that the council was a group of people who were chosen to represent different parts of the town – so this was their starting point.

1   The internet café was for everyone to use. Who do you think should make decisions about it? Explain why.

2   It is difficult for everyone to have a say on every topic. How might it be made simpler?

3   What sorts of decisions do you think should be made locally? Explain why.

Representing everyone

Akari, Emma and Steve had an issue that they wanted to discuss. The existing public loos were a waste of space which could be put to a better use. They needed to find the right people to talk to. They knew who the local councillor was – so this was the place to start.

The local **council** is made up of local people who make decisions about local services. These councillors represent different parts of the town, called wards. They are chosen in an election by the people who live in that **ward**.

In many areas, local elections take place every four years. **Political parties** put forward candidates for people to choose between. Each party will have already decided on a list of plans, called a **manifesto**. These plans will be put into practice if the party wins enough seats on the council.

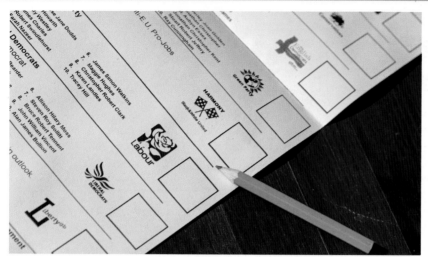

Sometimes there is a long list of people to choose from at an election. Some will represent the well-known political parties such as Labour, the Conservatives and the Liberal Democrats. Others will represent smaller groups like the Green party, or people who are independent of a party and are campaigning on a local issue. Most councils are a mix of political parties, but the party with most councillors takes overall control.

Almost everyone who is aged 18 or over can vote in these elections. Just like with the school council, the process is democratic because everyone can take part. Each year a form is sent to every house in the area to check who is entitled to vote.

Your vote is always secret, so nobody can check on your decision. Has your school or village hall ever been used as a **polling station** on election day?

Action

1 Find out who represents your area on the local council.

2 What is the mix of political parties that makes up your local council?

3 Find out about an issue that the council is discussing at the moment. What are the different points of view? Follow it up and find out what happens in the end.

Check your understanding

1 Who is on the local council?

2 How were these representatives chosen?

3 Why are most councils a mix of political parties?

4 Why do you think it is important that your vote is secret?

Another point of view

'Local decisions should be made by local people.'

Key terms

council: a group of people who are elected to look after the affairs of a town, district or county

manifesto: a published statement of the aims and policies of a political party

political party: an organised group of people with common aims who put up candidates for elections

polling station: a place where votes are cast; often a school, library or village hall

ward: an area that forms a separate part of a local council

Getting you thinking

Can do! 2

Steve, Emma and Akari set about finding out how to contact the people at the council who could help. They rang the main council switchboard and asked to talk to someone who could help them. They were put through to the Environment and Amenity Services department and explained their plan.

They were told that it would cost quite a lot, that the council had responsibilities to provide all sorts of other services and that money was short. They were told they should talk to the person who was responsible for community development.

They were also told they should talk to the members of the council's **cabinet** responsible for public toilets and community development. They decided that an email or letter might be the best way to make contact, because being a councillor is a spare-time job and councillors would be at work during the day. With the help of their local councillor, they set up a meeting to explain the plan.

1 Who makes decisions about local leisure and recreation issues?

2 What differences are there between the councillor and the person who works in the Environment and Amenity Services department?

3 Why do you think the council has to make choices between spending money on developing the public toilets and on other services, such as those for the elderly?

4 Why do you think the council listens to people who come to them with ideas about developing their community?

How is the council organised?

Every area of the country elects a councillor. When the council first meets after an election, it elects a leader and the members of the cabinet. The leader and cabinet all come from the political party that won the most votes: they have the **majority**.

Each member of the cabinet will have responsibility for one area of the council's work; for example, education, social services, finance, and leisure and recreation.

Apart from electing the cabinet, the council also elects overview and scrutiny committees to make sure the council is run properly.

Being a councillor carries a lot of responsibility, but the role is mainly voluntary. Councillors are paid travel expenses and an attendance fee for meetings, but they don't usually receive a salary.

How does the council do its work?

All the councillors meet to put together the plan for the year. They set the budget for each area of spending. The overview and scrutiny committees then make sure this plan is followed.

There are some areas, such as planning for things like housing and road building, that the council as a whole controls. Planning decisions are made according to laws laid down by central government, so the council sets up a committee to make sure that the rules are followed.

All councillors, whether they are members of the cabinet or not, must represent their ward in council decisions. They have a vote in council meetings and must use it in a way that serves their ward best.

As most of the officers on the council have full-time jobs, they cannot run the services as well. A **Chief Executive** is appointed to take responsibility for this. In each department, people who are experts in their field are employed to make sure it all runs smoothly.

The structure of the council

This is the most common structure for councils in the UK.

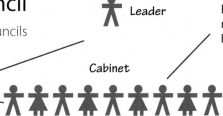

Leader

Each member of the cabinet is responsible for one area of the local council's work

Members of the party that won the most seats in the election

Cabinet

Other members of all political parties who have been elected to the council

Council

Committees

These people make recommendations to the cabinet about developments they would like to see in the area. The Scrutiny Committee checks up on the work of the cabinet.

What is a mayor?

In most places, a **mayor** has little power but takes part in local ceremonies. When the Queen or other famous people come to visit, the mayor puts on the chain of office and meets them. In May 2002, elections for directly elected mayors were held in a number of towns for the first time. Elected mayors have a lot more power, as London's mayor has shown.

Action

Have a look at your local council's website. Two example addresses are:
www.suffolkcc.gov.uk www.hullcc.gov.uk.

1 How is your council organised? Is there a cabinet and leader?

2 Which political party, if any, has control of your local council?

3 Find out about the work a councillor from your ward does.

4 Who would Steve, Emma and Akai have to talk to if the public loos were in your area?

Check your understanding

1 What does the council's cabinet do?

2 Who decides how much money to spend on each part of the council's work?

3 What do councillors do for their wards?

4 What's the difference between a councillor and a Chief Executive?

Another point of view

'The public loos should be converted.'

Key terms

cabinet: the main decision making body of the council

Chief Executive: an employee of the council, responsible for the smooth running of services

majority: the party with a majority has won a bigger proportion of the votes than the others

mayor: a member of the council who is selected to be its representative on ceremonial occasions; in some areas they are also the elected leader

Getting you thinking

1 Which of the services shown in the photos would you spend more money on? Explain why.

2 If you spend more on your choice, which services would you cut? Explain why.

3 If you decide not to cut anything, where would the money come from?

4 Why do councils often not want to spend more?

What does the council do?

Your local council is responsible for a range of services for your community, including education, social services, leisure, planning and transport, housing, fire and the police.

The amount of spending will depend on many different things. Here are some examples:

- If the population of the area is very young, they will need lots of schools.
- If there are many old people, they may need help from social services.
- If there are lots of people, there will be lots of refuse to collect.

A brand new sports centre, for example, is a very expensive item that has to be paid for. The council will work out how much it needs to spend in the coming year and then calculate how much money it must raise.

The council funds schools, which are free. It runs sports centres, which are usually cheaper than private clubs. The council provides these services because many people would not be able to afford to pay for them otherwise.

Sometimes councils work together with private businesses to run their services. Council houses can be sold to private housing associations, and councils can use the money to repair remaining council property or to build new council housing. Councils often pay businesses to run leisure facilities for them.

Central government sets a limit on how much money each council can spend, so the council has to work out its priorities. Councils never have the money to provide everything they would like to provide. When you vote in local elections, you are helping to decide what happens where you live.

A local council's income and expenditure (in £ million)

Expenditure

Social services £37.4

Fire and police £8.6

Planning and transport £12.8

Leisure £8.8

Housing £4.5

Other £6.7

Education £62.3

Income

Business rates £45.3

General government grant £26.1

Council tax £68

Tax surplus from last year £1.8

Where does the money come from?

In order to pay for these services, the local council raises money from residents and businesses in the area. Some of its income comes from charges for the services it provides. A large part of its spending comes from central government.

Council tax is paid by all the residents of the area. The amount that each person pays will depend on the value of the house they live in. People who live in bigger houses will pay more than those who live in smaller houses.

Business rates are paid by all the local businesses. The amount that is paid depends on the rent that could be charged for the office, shop or factory the business uses.

Central government contributes a major proportion of the money. The amount it contributes depends on the needs of the specific area and on how much can be raised locally. Poorer areas tend to receive more from central government than richer parts of the country.

Central government helps poorer areas more because it is harder for them to raise money locally. If many people are unemployed, houses will tend to have a lower value, so the council tax will only bring in a relatively small amount of money. Spending in these areas often needs to be greater because people who live there often need a lot of help from social services.

1 Make a list of services provided by this council. Put them in order according to how much they cost.

2 Why does the council spend money on these services?

3 If the council decided to spend more on leisure, where might the money come from?

Check your understanding

1 What sorts of services do local councils provide?

2 Where do local councils get their money from?

3 Why does central government give more money to some councils than to others?

4 Why is it important to vote in local elections?

Action

How does your local council raise and spend its money? You can find out from the town hall, council offices or the library. The council might also have a website with the information.

Another point of view

'Local taxation should be based on how much you earn instead of the value of your house.'

Key terms

business rates: a form of tax paid by all the businesses in an area. The amount a business pays depends on the rent that could be charged for its premises

council tax: a tax paid by everyone who lives in an area. It is based on the value of their house

1.22 Bringing it all together

Source A

Immigration and the nurses

The UK government is committed to reducing immigration. It ruled that people from outside the European Union could only stay in the UK if they earned more than £35 000 a year.

Only senior nurses earn as much as this, so 30 000 nurses would have faced being thrown out of the UK. This includes thousands from India.

The government came under pressure from the National Health Service because it was already being criticised for a shortage of nurses and poor care. As a result, the policy was changed so nurses joined the list of shortage jobs. This means that the new rule does not apply to them.

The change of policy came as a big relief to Indian nurses.

1. Which term describes nurses from India who come to work in the UK? *(1 mark)*
   A. ☐ asylum seekers
   B. ☑ economic migrants
   C. ☐ refugees
   D. ☐ dual heritage

2. Suggest two reasons why Indian nurses might want to come to work in the UK. *(2 marks)*

   1. They might want to come to the UK for better pay.

   2. They might want to come here because there are more opportunities.

   > There are many more reasons, including more training, a better standard of living or more up-to-date facilities. Remember, if there are two marks, you need to give two points.

3. Source A shows one way that the UK can benefit from immigration. Explain other ways in which the UK can benefit from immigration.

   Immigration helps the UK in many ways. People coming here often take jobs that people living here do not want to do — like fruit picking. This helps the economy, as we need people to do these jobs.

   Immigrants also bring different cultures to the UK. We now have restaurants selling all sorts of different food, and music from many different countries. This helps people in the UK to understand the way of life in many different places. It makes a difference to the society we live in.

   It also helps people learn to live in a diverse society, as they find out about people from other countries and how the same sorts of things are important to us all, wherever we come from.

Issues and debates

Source B

The Human Rights Act

The Human Rights Act is a UK law passed in 1998. It means that you can defend your rights in the UK courts and that public organisations (including the government, the police and local councils) must treat everyone equally, with fairness, dignity and respect.

The Human Rights Act protects all of us – young and old, rich and poor. Hopefully you will never need to rely on it, but every year hundreds of people do. Despite this, the government wants to replace our Human Rights Act with its British Bill of Rights. This would weaken everyone's rights – leaving politicians to decide when our fundamental freedoms should apply.

These are the same people who attacked open justice, destroyed legal aid and attacked Judicial Review.

We cannot let them take away our Human Rights Act too.

Source: Liberty

Source C

We will scrap the Human Rights Act

We will scrap Labour's Human Rights Act and introduce a British Bill of Rights, which will restore common sense to the application of human rights in the UK.

The Bill will remain faithful to the basic principles of human rights, which we signed up to in the original European Convention on Human Rights.

It will protect basic rights, like the right to a fair trial, and the right to life, which are an essential part of a modern democratic society.

But it will stop human rights law being used for more and more purposes, and often with little regard for the rights of wider society.

Among other things, the Bill will stop terrorists and other serious foreign criminals who pose a threat to our society from using bogus human rights arguments to prevent deportation.

Source: Conservative Manifesto 2015

1. Which of the following does Liberty say? *(1 mark)*
   A. ☐ The Human Rights Act affects very few people.
   B. ☑ Abolishing the Human Rights Act would give more power to Parliament.
   C. ☐ Abolishing the Human Rights Act would strengthen people's rights.
   D. ☐ A British Bill of Rights would strengthen our rights.

2. Which of the following does Conservative manifesto say? *(1 mark)*
   A. ☐ The Bill of Rights will be used for more legal purposes.
   B. ☐ The Human Rights Act has a common-sense approach.
   C. ☑ The Bill of Rights will protect the right to life.
   D. ☐ The Human Rights Act encourages deportation.

3. Analyse the sources to identify two views which the writers disagree about. *(2 marks)*

A British Bill of Rights will not protect us in the way the Human Rights Act does.

The Human Rights Act is used to protect people who are a threat to our society.

4. Which writer do you agree with more?
Explain your answer, referring to the arguments made in both sources. *(12 marks)*

I agree with the point of view of Liberty, which is a pressure group that aims to protect our human rights.

> The student is making a clear statement of their point of view and in the next paragraph uses the source to demonstrate the belief.

It requires that public organisations like the Government, the police and local councils must treat everyone equally, with fairness, dignity and respect. This is important if we are to live in a multicultural society in which people respect each other's way of life. There are many countries round the world where human rights are not respected and we do not want to live in a world like that.

> Here there is a wider perspective on the point of view.
> This is followed by reference to our role in Europe.

If our law is based on the European Convention on Human Rights, we will be in line with other European countries as they are all members of the Council of Europe. This will mean we are all subject to the same laws.

At the moment, judges decide whether people's human rights have not been respected. The Bill of Rights would mean that politicians could decide. If a law like this was passed, politicians might make decisions which promoted their views and restricted the views of other parties.

> This shows understanding of Liberty's reference to the effect of decisions being made by politicians.

The second view says that they would restore 'common sense' to how human rights are applied – but this is not very clear because people have different views about 'common sense'. It also mentions some human rights but doesn't mention others – so we really don't know what would not be included.

> The previous paragraph and the next one raise issues about the quality of the argument in both sources before winding up.

Although I support Liberty's view, the way they end their argument is not very strong. A party that is trying to save money because of the economy might cut spending on things like legal aid but might still believe in human rights.

Extended writing

'Integration is the only way community cohesion can be successful.'

How far do you agree with this view?

Give reasons for your opinion, showing that you have considered other points of view.

In your answer, you could consider:

* the effect of integration on identity
* ways of achieving community cohesion.

As integration means bringing different groups of people together in society, it is clearly very important if we are to have community cohesion. It will help to create a community where there is a sense of belonging and everyone from all communities and different backgrounds is valued. This is what is meant by community cohesion.

The student has shown that they understand the key terms used in the question.

The main fear is that people will lose their identity if integration goes too far and everyone is expected to be the same. Many people from different communities want to keep their identity. They want to pass on their language to their children so it is not forgotten. A Polish friend of mine, for example, is a member of a group that does traditional Polish dancing. I believe that it is important for people to keep their culture but still learn to fit in with our society in the UK.

This section starts to set out another point of view. This is essential if you want to get more than half marks.

There are all sorts of ways of encouraging people to take part in society while keeping their culture.

Here, the student is offering other ways of achieving community cohesion.

Schools are very good at doing this. Our school holds special days for different cultural groups within the school so we all learn about – and learn to respect – each other's traditions, but we all mix in together and everyone speaks English. Speaking English is very important if a diverse community is to work well together. It is difficult for someone who does not speak English to take part in society.

Local communities also organise events to bring communities together. The council in cities like Leicester, where there are many Asian families, runs festivals in the city to show everyone the culture and get people to come together and have fun.

The student has shown several different examples to support their argument.

All these methods mean that people are integrated but do not lose their identity. I agree that integration is good for community cohesion but it must be matched with activities that help people maintain their identity.

This makes clear where the student stands. This does not have to be on one side or the other. A good answer is often 'yes but ….'. The rest of the answer would develop the point of view.

Democracy at work in the UK

2.1 Getting elected

Getting you thinking

'Politics affects all of our lives in many ways, whether you're going through education, paying tax or seeking security in old age. I wanted to be a Member of Parliament because I wanted a fair society where everyone is considered and treated fairly. Changes in the law affect everyone from a newborn baby to an elderly person.

I was trying to buy my first house in Cornwall. At the time I was working as a postman and had a second job and was trying to save a deposit for a home. There were over 200 people bidding for affordable homes. We were lucky to get one.

'I listened to the Prime Minister's first speech after the **general election**. He outlined what the government would do differently. He talked about cutting taxes for working people, removing unnecessary laws which were restricting business growth, and making it easier for people to keep more of the money they earn. It was at this point I realised I wanted to be involved in the party.'

Scott Mann worked as a postman, before he got into politics

1 What made Scott decide to become an MP?

2 Why did Scott decide to join a political party?

3 Why does Scott think people should have their say?

4 What issues do politicians deal with?

Becoming a Member of Parliament

There are 650 Members of Parliament, or MPs. They have all been elected to represent a part of the country known as a constituency. If you want to become an MP, you need to be selected in a competitive process. The parties have different ways of doing this but, in general, you have to put yourself forward, be selected by the parties and then offer yourself to a constituency which you would like to represent. There will be interviews and **hustings**, where you have to stand up and explain what you believe and why you want to be the MP for this constituency. If the party members like what they hear, you will be selected to be their candidate. If you win the election, you then become the MP who represents everyone in the area.

A few people stand as independents and therefore do not go through the party system. This was the case with a doctor, Richard Taylor, who was furious that the local hospital was to be closed; he stood as an independent and won the seat.

Fighting an election

You have all seen posters everywhere at election time. A general election takes place every five years. The political parties know when it is going to be and plan well ahead.

To attract voters, the political parties and candidates will:

- send out leaflets telling people what they have done in the past and plan to do in future

- go **canvassing**

- attract press coverage

- hold public meetings.

There is a limit on how much parties can spend on electioneering.

What sort of democracy?

The UK is a **representative democracy**, so everyone who is entitled to vote takes part. We elect people who make decisions for us. **Direct democracy** is another system in which everyone votes on every issue through a **referendum**. This is how democracy started, but it gets very difficult to run in countries with large populations.

You will discover how an MP gets elected to the House of Commons and learn how the electoral system works.

2.1 Getting elected

Who can vote?

To vote in a UK general election you must be registered. This means being on the electoral register. If you are 18 years of age or more on polling day and a British citizen, a citizen of most Commonwealth countries or the Republic of Ireland, you will be able to vote.

The law states that you will not be able to vote if you:

- are a member of the House of Lords
- are an EU citizen resident in the UK
- are a convicted prisoner
- have been found guilty of corrupt practices in an election in the last five years.

There are arguments in the UK for young people over the age of 16 to have the vote. They were eligible to vote in the Scottish Referendum in 2014. Many people think that 16-year-olds are capable of making such decisions, but not all political parties favour it.

Votes at 16

Soila said: 'At 16, I may have a job, be married or have a child. 16-year-olds who work have to pay tax and we all pay VAT on things we buy. The government then spends that tax on what they choose. Shouldn't we play a part in deciding who has that responsibility?'

Counting the votes

In a general election, the system used in the UK is known as **first past the post**. It takes place when a single MP is elected to one **constituency**. When you vote, you put a cross in a box next to the candidate you would like to be elected. The candidate with the most votes in the constituency wins.

Action

1 Who is your local MP? Which political party do they belong to?

2 How many candidates were there at the last election in your constituency? Which parties did they represent? How many votes did each candidate win?

Check your understanding

1 How many MPs are there in the House of Commons?

2 What is the name for the area represented by an MP?

3 Do all candidates represent one of the main political parties? Explain your answer.

4 How do candidates try to attract voters?

Another point of view

'The voting age should be 16.'

Key Terms

canvassing: when people try to persuade others to vote for their party in an election

constituency: the area represented by an MP

direct democracy: a form of democracy in which everyone votes on every decision in a referendum

first past the post: an electoral system where voters have one vote in their constituency and the candidate with the most votes wins

general election: an election for a new government. In the UK, these take place at least every five years

hustings: a meeting at which candidates in an election speak to the voters

referendum: a vote by the whole electorate on a particular issue

representative democracy: a form of democracy in which people elect a representative to make decisions for them

2.2 Does everyone's vote count?

Getting you thinking

At the general election in 2015 there was a big difference in the percentage of votes cast for each party and the percentage of seats won. The votes and the 650 seats in the UK Parliament were allocated as follows.

1 Does this seem fair?

2 Approximately how many seats should each party have if the votes were allocated fairly?

3 Can you think of a way that would be fairer and ensure that everyone's vote counts?

Party	Votes won (%)	Seats won (%)	Seats won
Conservative	36.9	51	331
Labour	30.5	36	232
UKIP	12.6	0	1
Lib Dems	7.8	1	8
SNP	4.7	9	56
Green	3.8	0	1

Which voting system?

First past the post

As you learned on page 57, first past the post (FPTP) is used in UK general elections. It has both advantages and disadvantages.

The **advantages** of FPTP are:

- Extremist parties are unlikely to be elected as they won't be able to win enough votes in any one constituency.

- The result becomes clear very quickly, so the winning party can take over government as soon as the election is over.

The **disadvantages** of FPTP are:

- The number of votes cast for a party does not reflect the number of seats won. A party can win an election with a minority of the votes.

- Smaller parties tend to win few seats because they don't have enough support in each constituency.

- People may vote tactically to keep a party out rather than for the party they believe in.

Proportional representation

Proportional representation (PR) means that the number of seats a party wins is roughly proportional to the votes it receives in an election.

There are many different sorts of PR, but they all work in this way. In the simplest example, you have a large constituency and a list of candidates. You might vote for the candidate or the list, but each votes counts.

The **advantages** of PR are:

- no votes are wasted

- the number of seats the parties win reflects the percentage of votes cast for each party.

The **disadvantages** of PR are:

- it is difficult to stand as an independent candidate.

- the party can draw up the list of candidates so only people who agree with the powerful people in a party will be elected. This is not good for democracy.

- the elected MP has no local link in a big constituency.

- small parties can have unfair power over the larger parties by threatening to withdraw from a coalition.

You will learn about the advantages and disadvantages of different voting systems.

2.2 Does everyone's vote count?

Elections for the European Parliament

Every five years, there are elections for the European Parliament. In the UK we elect 73 Members of the European Parliament (**MEP**s). They are elected in Great Britain and Northern Ireland.

There are 12 electoral regions in the UK, as shown on the map. Each region has between 3 and 10 MEPs.

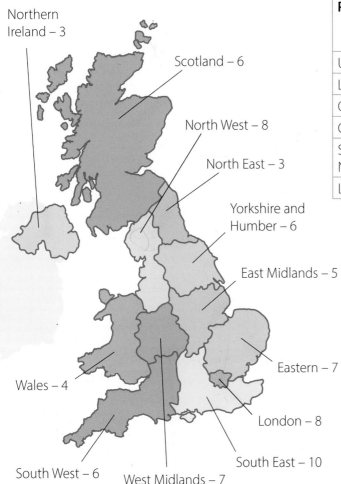

Northern Ireland – 3
Scotland – 6
North West – 8
North East – 3
Yorkshire and Humber – 6
East Midlands – 5
Eastern – 7
Wales – 4
London – 8
South East – 10
South West – 6
West Midlands – 7

MEPs are elected in England, Scotland and Wales by a system of PR known as the **closed-list system**. Each party in each region puts forward a list of people in the order they will be selected.

The ballot paper shows the parties' names and lists their candidates. Any independent candidates are listed at the end. The voter puts a cross next to the party or independent candidate they wish to vote for.

In 2014, there was an election for MEPs. In 2015, there was a UK general election. The outcomes were very different.

As the constituencies were larger, the votes for UKIP across the regions added up to many more seats.

European Election 2014		UK General Election 2015	
Party	**Elected MEPs of 73**	**Party**	**Elected MPs of 650**
UKIP	24	Conservative	331
Labour	20	Labour	232
Conservatives	19	Scottish Nationalists	56
Green	3	Liberal Democrats	8
Scottish Nationalists	2	Green	1
Liberal Democrats	1	UKIP	1

Check your understanding

1 What does FPTP stand for?

2 What does PR stand for?

3 What are the advantages and disadvantages of FPTP?

4 What are the advantages and disadvantages of PR?

5 Which electoral system is used for European elections in England, Scotland and Wales?

6 Is the same system used everywhere in Europe?

Another point of view

'Proportional representation must be used for all UK elections.'

Key Terms

closed-list system: a form of PR in which a party puts forward a list of candidates in the order they will be elected

MEP: Member of the European Parliament

proportional representation: an electoral system in which the number of seats a party wins is roughly proportional to its share of the votes in an election

2.3 Who shall I vote for?

Getting you thinking

Which paper do you read?

Newspapers let people know what's going on, but they can also affect the way people think. Some newspapers always reflect the ideas of one of the political parties, while others take a wider view.

What's your age, gender and ethnicity?

More young people and ethnic minorities vote Labour. More women used to vote Conservative, but the balance has now shifted.

Which social class are you in?

Upper- and middle-class people have tended to vote Conservative and working-class people to vote Labour. However, this divide has become less rigid as the parties' policies have become more alike and society has become less class-based.

Do you like the party's policies and image?

People tend to vote for the party as a whole rather than their local candidate. The image of the party and its leader has become increasingly important as the role of the media has increased.

What do your friends think?

People's decisions on who to vote for are often affected by their friends and family.

What's your religion?

Religious beliefs can persuade people to vote for the party that holds views in line with their own.

Where do you live?

Political parties often have strongholds in certain areas. For instance, in the South East more people have traditionally voted Conservative.

1 Select two of these factors and explain how they affect people's decision on which party to vote for.

2 How do you think the political parties use this information to persuade people to vote for their candidates?

3 Why can having lots of money help a party to win votes?

Which party?

At the last general election, 61 parties put forward candidates. Some of the parties are very small or very local. They include The Pirate Party, Justice for Men and Boys, and We Are The Reality Party. None of these won a seat in Parliament. Only 11 parties won seats and the vast majority were won by just two parties, the Conservative Party and the Labour Party.

The range of parties means that there is the opportunity for many different points of view to be voiced. Freedom of speech is an important right in the UK.

The decision you make is very important because the party that is elected will run the country for the next five years. The laws that are passed and the decisions that are made about raising taxes and spending money on the services the government provides all depend on the party that is elected.

You will think about the differences between the main political parties.

2.3 Who shall I vote for?

What's the difference?

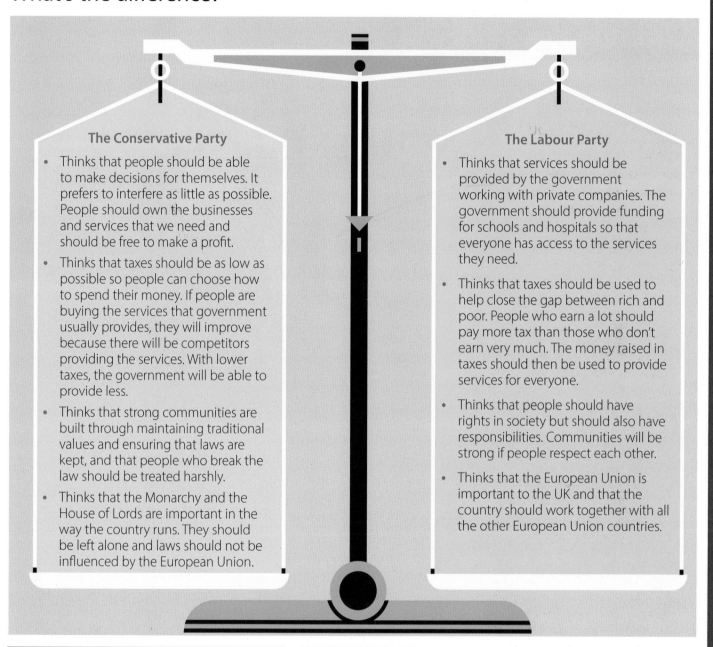

The Conservative Party

- Thinks that people should be able to make decisions for themselves. It prefers to interfere as little as possible. People should own the businesses and services that we need and should be free to make a profit.

- Thinks that taxes should be as low as possible so people can choose how to spend their money. If people are buying the services that government usually provides, they will improve because there will be competitors providing the services. With lower taxes, the government will be able to provide less.

- Thinks that strong communities are built through maintaining traditional values and ensuring that laws are kept, and that people who break the law should be treated harshly.

- Thinks that the Monarchy and the House of Lords are important in the way the country runs. They should be left alone and laws should not be influenced by the European Union.

The Labour Party

- Thinks that services should be provided by the government working with private companies. The government should provide funding for schools and hospitals so that everyone has access to the services they need.

- Thinks that taxes should be used to help close the gap between rich and poor. People who earn a lot should pay more tax than those who don't earn very much. The money raised in taxes should then be used to provide services for everyone.

- Thinks that people should have rights in society but should also have responsibilities. Communities will be strong if people respect each other.

- Thinks that the European Union is important to the UK and that the country should work together with all the other European Union countries.

Actions

- Look at the Labour and Conservative parties' websites and find out more about their policies: www.labour.org.uk and www.conservatives.com

- Think carefully about which party's views you prefer and explain why. You can use the Vote for Policies website to help you work out which party has policies you agree with: https://voteforpolicies.org.uk

Check your understanding

1 How are people influenced when they vote?

2 What are the main features of the Labour and Conservative parties' beliefs?

3 Why do you think there are so many political parties in the UK?

Another point of view

'The UK only needs one political party.'

2.4 Into power

Getting you thinking

Scott outside the Houses of Parliament on his first day as MP for North Cornwall

'On 8 May 2015 I became the MP for North Cornwall. On the Monday of the following week I made my first walk across Westminster Bridge and into the Houses of Parliament. It was a very special moment for me to look at the Palace of Westminster and think, 'I have changed my job from a postman in Cornwall to an MP in London'.

The Houses of Parliament are full of so much history statues of former Prime Ministers, beautiful buildings and famous MPs who I had only previously seen on television. In my own way I am now a small part of that history. It's my aim to speak up for North Cornwall and support the country and its people for as long as the people of our great nation keep electing me.'

1 Why was entering the House of Commons such a special moment for Scott?

2 What might you think if you had become an MP and entered the House of Commons for the first time?

3 What did Scott want to do once he had become an MP?

4 If you had just become an MP, what would you like to change?

After the election

The leader of the party with the most seats will be called to see the Monarch. A question will be posed: 'Can you form a government?' If the answer is 'Yes', the leader of the winning party will become the new Prime Minister.

It is the Monarch's responsibility to appoint the new Prime Minister, but this is carried out with advice from others. The Monarch must never take sides.

Once appointed, the Prime Minister must set about selecting who will be in the **Cabinet**. These are people who run the most important work of the government. You will find out more on page 64.

Sometimes the election results are not clear and no party has a clear majority. The parties have to work out how they can work together. There may be long talks between the parties to decide which group of parties will form the government. In 2010, the Conservatives and Liberal Democrats decided to work together, so they formed a **coalition**. They had enough seats together to have a majority and could therefore form the government.

Taking your seat

For a new MP, taking your seat in the House of Commons is an exciting event. After what might be years of wanting and waiting to be elected, joining the body that runs the country is a big moment.

MPs debate new laws and policies in the House of Commons. Sometimes debates become furious and the **Speaker** has to act very firmly to keep things in order. On occasion, an MP can be temporarily thrown out of the House of Commons if things get out of hand. MPs generally vote with the party to which they belong, but sometimes they follow their conscience.

The Speaker is an MP, chosen by the rest to organise business and keep order.

Backbench MPs, who don't have jobs in the government or **opposition**, sit on benches at the back.

The government benches: the **Prime Minister** sits at the front, surrounded by the Cabinet.

The opposition benches: the Leader of the opposition sits at the front, surrounded by the **Shadow Cabinet**.

MPs who don't belong to the main party or largest opposition party also sit on the opposition bench.

Starting work

MPs have a range of responsibilities.

Their first responsibility is to the people who elected them. There is often a lot of mail from the constituency, which must be dealt with. An MP will hold a frequent 'surgery' in the constituency to listen to people's ideas and worries. They take part in debates in the House of Commons and will usually vote with their political party.

If they have a post in a government department, they will be busy working on government policy and working out new laws.

They might sit on a committee that keeps a check on the activities of the government departments.

Ministers are know as **front benchers**. Other MPs are called **back benchers** because of where they sit in the **House of Commons**.

The opposition sits facing the government. It has the same organisation as the government, with a Shadow Cabinet.

Check your understanding

1   What is the responsibility of every MP?

2. What does the Queen ask the leader of the winning party?

3. What happens if the answer is 'Yes'?

4. What is a coalition?

Another point of view

'MPs should always vote with the party they belong to.'

Key Terms

back benchers: MPs who do not hold office in the government or opposition; they sit on the back benches in the House of Commons

Cabinet: a group of MPs who head major government departments. It meets weekly to make decisions about how government policy will be carried out. Senior Ministers from the Lords are also represented

coalition: a government made of more than one party. It is formed when no one party has enough seats to form a government

front benchers: MPs who hold office in the government or opposition. They sit on the front benches in the House of Commons

House of Commons: the more powerful of the two parts of the British Parliament. Its members are elected by the public

opposition: political parties that are not in power

Prime Minister: the leader of the majority party in the House of Commons and the leader of the government

Shadow Cabinet: MPs from the main opposition party who 'shadow' MPs who head major government departments

Speaker: the MP elected to act as chairman for debates in the House of Commons

2.5 Forming a government

Getting you thinking

Apart from Larry, the Downing Street cat, you have to be invited by the Prime Minister to take a seat in the Cabinet.

The Cabinet is the group of MPs who lead the most important government departments such as finance, health, education and defence. The Prime Minister has to choose very carefully so the best people take the jobs.

The Cabinet meets weekly in the Cabinet Room to decide on government policy and make important decisions.

1 Look at the list of government departments below. Which do you think should be represented in the Cabinet?

2 What skills do you think a Cabinet minister should have?

3 If you were Prime Minister, how would you set about selecting your Cabinet?

What does the Prime Minister do?

Apart from setting up the government, the Prime Minister has several other important roles. These include:

- directing government policy
- managing the Cabinet
- organising government
- controlling Parliament
- providing national leadership.

The Cabinet and other ministers

The Cabinet is the inner circle of ministers. It is involved in all serious decision making. It includes:

- the Treasury, which runs the finances
- the Home Office, which is responsible for protecting the public
- the Foreign and Commonwealth Affairs Office, which is responsible for the UK's interests abroad.

Other departments in the Cabinet are usually:

- health
- defence
- justice

- children, schools and families
- culture, media and sport
- business and enterprise
- environment, food and rural affairs
- transport
- international development.

Wales, Scotland and Northern Ireland also have their own departments. The people who lead these departments are known as **Secretaries of State**. They have assistants called **Ministers of State**. There is also a range of other jobs for non-Cabinet MPs in the departments. Each department has a staff of civil servants who develop and carry out its policies.

After the election, MPs wait for a call from the Prime Minister's office, in the hope of getting a job in the government. Getting the first job in a government department is a step to becoming a Minister.

A new government

Once the government has been formed, the Prime Minister and Cabinet decide on their plans for the next five years. These are announced in the Queen's – or King's – Speech when the Monarch opens the new sitting of Parliament. The Queen or King comes to Parliament and makes the speech from the House of Lords.

The two houses

Parliament is **bi-cameral** as it has two 'houses'.

- the House of Commons ,which is elected
- the House of Lords, which is both appointed and hereditary.

MPs are called to the House of Lords by **Black Rod**, who looks after the Palace of Westminster as The Houses of Parliament is known.

When Black Rod arrives at the House of Commons, the doors are slammed in his face. This is to show the independence of the House of Commons from the Monarch. Black Rod knocks three times and the MPs are allowed in to hear the speech.

Black Rod knocks on the door of the House of Commons.

Complete power?

The UK Prime Minister has much power but, whatever the government plans, Parliament will have its say and the Monarch has to sign it off.

The diagram below shows who does what. The Monarch sits at the top, but generally only acts on the advice of others. The roles shown in the diagram are not completely separate as they frequently work together. You will find out more on page 70.

	Monarch		
	Legislature	**Executive**	**Judiciary**
What do they do?	Makes law	Draws up and puts policy into action	Makes judgments about the law
Who is involved?	House of Commons House of Lords	Prime Minister Cabinet Civil Service	Judge and magistrates in courts

You will find out more on page 70.

Check your understanding

1 What does the Prime Minister do?
2 What do the following ministries do?
   - The Treasury
   - The Home Office
   - The Foreign and Commonwealth Affairs Office
3 What is the difference between a Secretary of State and a Minister of State?
4 What does bi-cameral mean?
5 What do the following do?
   - The Legislature
   - The Executive
   - The Judiciary

Another point of view

'The Prime Minister is too powerful. There are not enough checks on what's being done.'

Key Terms

bi-cameral: the UK Parliament is bi-cameral because it has two Houses, the House of Commons and the House of Lords

Black Rod: the person who has ceremonial duties in the Palace of Westminster, including bringing MPs to the House of Lords for the State Opening of Parliament

the executive: makes policy and puts it into practice. It is made up of the Prime Minister, Cabinet and Civil Service

the judiciary: makes judgments about the law. It is made up of judges and magistrates in courts

the legislature: makes laws. It is made up of the House of Lords and House of Commons

Minister of State: an assistant to the Secretary of State

Secretary of State: an MP who is in charge of a government department such as health or defence

2.6 How are laws made?

Getting you thinking

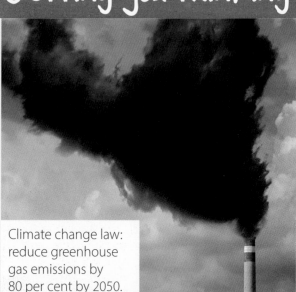

Climate change law: reduce greenhouse gas emissions by 80 per cent by 2050.

The Community Rehabilitation Order aims to:
- ensure that the young person takes responsibility for his/her crime
- help the young person to resolve any personal difficulties that may have contributed to his/her offending
- help the young person become a law-abiding and responsible member of the community.

Smoking in cars carrying children is now illegal.

School-leaving age: from 2015, everyone will have to stay in education or training until 18.

1 Why do you think the government wanted to make laws like these?

2 What, in your opinion, would happen if the government passed laws that the population did not like?

3 Why do people, in general, keep the laws that are passed by Parliament?

Power

Parliament passes laws that determine how we live our lives. By electing a government, we give it the power to do this. If people break the laws, they can be punished. The government is given authority because the population accepts that an election is a fair way of deciding who will hold power for a five-year period.

The government is **accountable** because it has to answer to the voters. If voters do not like what is happening, the government will not be re-elected.

How are laws made?

Laws go through several stages before coming into force. The government often puts out a **Green Paper**, which puts forward ideas for future laws. Once the ideas have

been made final, a **White Paper** is published. This lays out the government's policy. To turn policy into law, the proposals are introduced to Parliament in the form of a **bill**. To change the school-leaving age, for example, the government would have to introduce an Education Bill. Having gone through the process shown in the diagram on the page opposite, the bill becomes an **Act of Parliament** and, therefore, part of the law of the country. The government is accountable to the population, so it needs to be sure that everyone has had an opportunity to comment.

It is important that laws are put together, or 'drafted' carefully, because there are always some people who want to find a way of avoiding them. If a law can be interpreted in a different way, it will be very hard to enforce. The law to ban hunting, for example, is proving difficult to enforce.

The debate

Most bills are introduced by the government. Sometimes the parties are in agreement and all goes smoothly, but often the opposition seriously disagrees either on the policy as a whole or on aspects of it. This leads to lengthy debate when the opposition tries to persuade the government to accept changes – or amendments – to the bill.

Passing through Parliament

First reading
The bill is introduced formally in the House of Commons. Before it reaches this stage, it has been worked on by a drafting committee to make sure that it is put together correctly. A bill can be many pages long. At this stage there is no debate.

Second reading
A few weeks after the first reading stage, the bill is debated fully in the House of Commons. A vote is taken and, if the majority of MPs approve of the bill, it is passed.

Standing committee
A group of 16 to 20 MPs looks at the bill carefully and makes any alterations that came up at the second reading, or which they now think are appropriate.

Report stage
The committee sends a report to the House of Commons with all its amendments. These amendments are either approved or changed. Changes are made when there is a lot of opposition to the bill or if there is strong public pressure to make changes.

House of Lords
The bill goes through the same process as in the Commons. If the Lords want to change anything, the bill is returned to the Commons.

Third reading
The amended bill is presented to the House of Commons. A debate is held and a vote is taken on whether to approve it.

Royal assent
Once the bill has passed all its stages in the Commons and the Lords, it is sent to the Queen for her signature. This is really a formality, as the Queen would never refuse to sign a bill that had been through the democratic process. The bill then becomes an Act of Parliament and part of the law of the country.

Action

Choose a new law that you would like to see passed. Put your proposals into a 'bill'. Work out what the opposition is likely to say and prepare your arguments.

Check your understanding

1   What is the difference between a bill and an Act?

2   What sort of things do committees have to pay attention to when making amendments to bills?

3   Why do you think there are so many stages before a law is made?

Key Terms

accountable: if you are accountable for something, you are responsible for it and have to explain your actions

Act of Parliament: a law passed by Parliament

bill: a proposal to change something into law

Green Paper: this puts forward ideas that the government wants discussed before it starts to develop a policy

White Paper: this puts government policy up for discussion before it becomes law

Getting you thinking

Here are two views on how to vote in the 2014 referendum on Scotland's independence.

Yes!

'A "Yes" vote means we can choose to have power over our country's future – and make Scotland a better place to live for all of us.

Even our opponents agree that Scotland has what it takes to be a successful independent country. An independent Scotland would be among the 20 wealthiest nations in the world. But we need independence to make that wealth work better for the people who live here by creating more and better jobs.'

No!

'A "No" vote will mean a better future for my kids. They will have more job opportunities and better funding for schools and hospitals.

Most people I have talked to think that devolution has been a success. The decisions made in Scotland are guaranteed because of our links with England. There is the power to raise money for our NHS, to help people back to work, and look after welfare. We can have progress in Scotland without the risks of separation.'

1 Set out the two arguments for and against Scottish independence.
2 What is the difference between devolution and independence?
3 Do you think Scotland should become independent?

Devolution

The Scottish Parliament and Welsh **Assembly** were both set up following referenda in 1998. There had been lengthy campaigns for **devolution** in both countries. People wanted devolution because it shifted some power and authority from London to their own capital cities.

The extent to which power is shared with Westminster varies according to the strength of the vote in the referendum in each country.

Scotland voted strongly for its Parliament, which has the ability to raise taxes and pass laws. There are constant debates about how much power the Parliament should have. This was brought to a head in a referendum in 2014 when the Scots were asked if they wanted independence. The vote was narrowly lost but the Scottish Parliament was given considerably more power over taxation, elections and social policy such as drugs and drink driving.

The powers of the Scottish Parliament:

- agriculture, fisheries and forestry
- economic development
- education
- environment
- food standards
- health
- home affairs
- law – courts, police, fire services
- local government
- research and statistics
- social work
- sport and the arts
- tourism
- training
- transport.

The Scottish Parliament chamber

The Welsh Assembly chamber

The **Welsh** voted by a narrow margin of 0.6 per cent for their Assembly. The Welsh Assembly can spend the UK government's allocation of money to Wales, but it cannot set taxes and has limited law-making powers.

Northern Ireland's Assembly was set up in 1998 but has often been suspended because of disagreement among Irish politicians. The current Assembly has powers to control education, health, local government, policing and justice.

There are calls for regional assemblies in the rest of the UK too. Many people in regions such as Cornwall feel that their part of the country is distinctive and has different needs from the rest of the UK. People in the North East, however, rejected the idea when a referendum was held. The cost of running a regional assembly was one factor in their decision.

The effect of the changes

The more powers that are transferred to the Scottish Parliament, the more some people in England want to change the way Scottish MPs vote in Westminster. They question whether Scottish MPs should be allowed to vote on issues that affect only England, since English MPs can't vote on the same issues in Scotland.

Check your understanding

1   What is the purpose of a referendum? When is one held?

2   What is devolution?

4   What's the difference in the amount of power held by the Scottish Parliament and the Welsh Assembly?

5   Why do some Scottish people want independence?

6   Why do some people want to have regional governments?

Action

The Scottish referendum on independence resulted in the decision to stay in the UK. There was, however, still pressure for change. Check up on what is happening and how the powers of the Scottish Parliament are changing.

Another point of view

'Devolution means that better decisions are made for a region because they are made locally.'

Key Terms

Assembly: a body of people elected to decide on some areas of spending in a region

devolution: the transfer of power from central to regional government

Getting you thinking

A constitution? Don't you trust me?

Before Magna Carta, the Monarch had complete control over what happened in the country. King John was forced to sign Magna Carta and hand over some power to the barons. This was the beginning of the British constitution.

1 What might happen today if there were no rules about the actions of the Monarch or Prime Minister?

2 Why is trust not enough?

3 Think of examples of what happens in countries where leaders do not accept the country's constitution – if there is one.

What is the British constitution?

The **British constitution** sets out how we are governed. Many countries have a written constitution, but the UK's is not written down. It is a set of rules which lay down how much power the government has, when elections must be held and the influence the Monarch can have.

It all comes from a number of sources, which together tell us how the country should be run.

The British constitution is not set in stone. As the law changes, it is incorporated into the constitution. Membership of the European Union has meant that laws passed by the European Parliament affect British Law. Devolution within the UK also changes the way our Parliament works.

Parliamentary sovereignty

Parliamentary sovereignty is the most important part of the Constitution. It means that Parliament is the chief source of law in the UK. The government must be drawn from Parliament and it cannot pass laws that can't be changed by future Parliaments.

Conventions tell us a range of things that have developed over time – for example, that the Prime Minister should be in the House of Commons. This was not always the case.

British constitution

Common law is made by judges. When they make decisions in court they sometimes change the law. See page 67.

European law affects the UK as a member of the European Union.

Statute law is law that has been passed by Parliament over a long period. These laws start with Magna Carta and, in more recent times, include Britain's joining the European Community, devolution when the Scottish Parliament was set up, and the introduction of the Human Rights Act.

Are there checks and balances on Parliament?

The way that the branches of government are kept separate means that each one keeps a check on the others. On page 65, you learned about the legislature, executive and judiciary, which set out these three areas of government and why it is important that they are independent.

Judicial review is a further check. A court's decision can be challenged if it is suspected that it has not been properly made. Here are some examples of the sort of decisions that are challenged:

- local government decisions about welfare benefits and special education
- immigration decisions about whether people can stay in the country
- decisions about prisoners' rights.

Select committees also check up on the work of Parliament. Every government department has a select committee that watches over the decisions it makes. They gather evidence and produce reports. Each department has 60 days to reply to the comments of its select committee.

Parliamentary inquiries can be requested if there is concern that the government isn't doing something properly. The Children's Society, for example, requested an enquiry on the care of children of asylum seekers. The report it produced gave advice to the government on changes that should be made.

Judicial review: Snibston Discovery Museum

Leicester County Council decided to close the Snibston Discovery Museum because it said it could no longer afford to run it.

The Friends of Snibston Museum really wanted to keep the museum open. They asked for a judicial review. They said that the consultation the council had carried out was not good enough. The question that had been asked made it hard for people to disagree with closing the museum, so it had not been done properly. The judge agreed that the judicial review should go ahead. When it did, the verdict was that the Council was right and the museum could close.

Check your understanding

1 What is the British constitution?

2 What makes up the British constitution?

3 Are there checks and balances on the government? What are they?

4 Explain how a judicial review works.

Another point of view

'The government has been elected by everyone so must not be challenged.'

Key Terms

British constitution: the laws and conventions which set down how the UK is governed

judicial review: a review carried out by the High Court to decide whether a decision made by a public body has been made properly

Parliamentary inquiry: an enquiry set up to investigate actions taken by government departments and public bodies

Parliamentary sovereignty: Parliament is the top legal body and can pass new laws or stop old laws

select committee: one of the committees that check and report on the work of government departments

Theme B: Democracy at work in the UK

Getting you thinking

My mum got a grant to go to university but I'm going to end up with enormous debts.

I live on my own and I haven't any children. Why should I pay all these taxes for schools and the elderly?

I've tried and tried to get another job. I just reckon I'm too old. They think I'm not trying and say my benefits will be cut.

I just can't make ends meet. Why can't the government give us enough pension to live on?

1 What are these people worried about?

2 Make a list of the areas of spending which the questions refer to.

3 Where do you think the money comes from to pay for all these services?

4 Do you think there is a limit to the amount the government can spend? Why?

5 How should the government decide how to spend its money?

What does the government spend?

The government spends its money on a wide range of services. The pie chart below shows the main areas of spending and the proportion spent on each area. The way it is divided up varies a little from year to year but the overall picture stays much the same.

Total managed expenditure: £742 billion

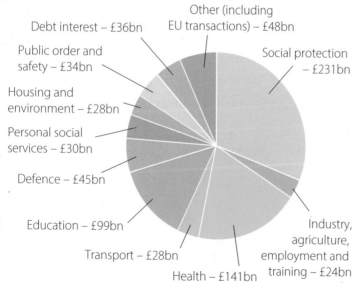

- Other (including EU transactions) – £48bn
- Debt interest – £36bn
- Public order and safety – £34bn
- Housing and environment – £28bn
- Personal social services – £30bn
- Defence – £45bn
- Education – £99bn
- Transport – £28bn
- Health – £141bn
- Social protection – £231bn
- Industry, agriculture, employment and training – £24bn

Source: HM Treasury

Where does the money come from?

If the government is to provide these services, it needs to raise money to pay for them. The money, or **government revenue**, comes from taxation or borrowing, as the pie chart below shows.

Total revenue: £673 billion

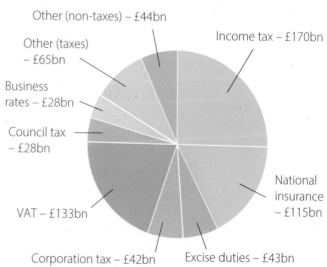

- Other (non-taxes) – £44bn
- Other (taxes) – £65bn
- Business rates – £28bn
- Council tax – £28bn
- VAT – £133bn
- Corporation tax – £42bn
- Income tax – £170bn
- National insurance – £115bn
- Excise duties – £43bn

Source: HM Treasury

What taxes?

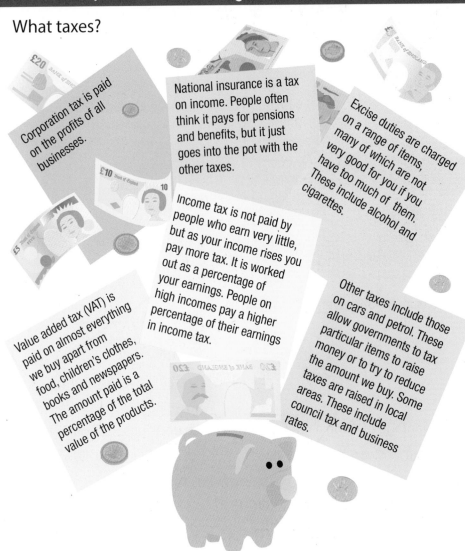

Corporation tax is paid on the profits of all businesses.

National insurance is a tax on income. People often think it pays for pensions and benefits, but it just goes into the pot with the other taxes.

Excise duties are charged on a range of items, many of which are not very good for you if you have too much of them. These include alcohol and cigarettes.

Income tax is not paid by people who earn very little, but as your income rises you pay more tax. It is worked out as a percentage of your earnings. People on high incomes pay a higher percentage of their earnings in income tax.

Value added tax (VAT) is paid on almost everything we buy apart from food, children's clothes, books and newspapers. The amount paid is a percentage of the total value of the products.

Other taxes include those on cars and petrol. These allow governments to tax particular items to raise money or to try to reduce the amount we buy. Some taxes are raised in local areas. These include council tax and business rates.

Making ends meet

The decisions on taxes and spending happen each year in the **Budget**. The **Chancellor of the Exchequer** is responsible for deciding where the money comes from and how it is spent. The Chancellor works with government departments to decide what is needed and what must come first. It can be difficult to get the right balance, because often every department will want to spend more.

Just like everyone else, if the government wants to spend more than its income, it has to borrow money. When it borrows, it has to pay interest to the people who lend it the money. When the Chancellor makes decisions on the amount of tax raised, expenditure and borrowing, the risks involved have to be weighed up.

Over the years, there has been a steady increase in the amount that governments spend. At the moment, it amounts to about £10 000 per person, per year. People's voting decisions often depend on what the political parties say they will do about taxes and spending if they win the election.

Check your understanding

1 What does the Chancellor of the Exchequer do? Why can this work be difficult?

2 Explain the different types of taxation that the government uses to raise money.

3 What has been happening to the amount of government spending over the years?

4 Why might government spending influence the way people vote?

Action

The Treasury is the government department responsible for the Budget. Look at its website at https://www.gov.uk/government/organisations/hm-treasury to find out how the government raises and spends its money. Click on the 'Budget' heading on the site. You will find documents that explain the government's spending decisions.

Another point of view

'If the NHS wants more money, it should get it.'

Key Terms

Budget: the process each year when the Chancellor of the Exchequer explains how the government will raise and spend its money

Chancellor of the Exchequer: the member of the government who is responsible for the country's finances

government revenue: the money raised by the government

2.10 Bringing it all together

Source A

The future of the UK

In September 2014, people in Scotland were asked whether they wanted to become independent from the UK. They voted in a referendum, which had a very high turnout. The result was that 45 per cent voted to leave the UK and 55 per cent voted to stay.

In order to persuade Scottish people to vote to stay, the UK government gave Scotland greater powers over its own affairs. The powers included taxation, elections and social policy such as drugs and drink driving.

The interest in the Scottish referendum led to people in Wales wanting more powers. They already have an Assembly but feel like second-class citizens when compared with the Scots. The UK parliament suggested that more powers would be transferred to Wales as a result.

1. Which term is used to describe the transfer of powers to Scotland? *(1 mark)*

   ☐ Proportional representation
   ☑ Devolution
   ☐ Integration
   ☐ Advocacy

2. Give one advantage and one disadvantage of using a referendum to make decisions. *(2 marks)*

   Advantage: A referendum gives a clear answer on a single question.

   Disadvantage: It cannot not be used for every decision a government has to make.

3. Source A discusses the transfer of powers from the UK parliament to Scotland. Explain how the transfer of powers to the countries that make up the UK affects England. *(6 marks)*

   As the countries of the UK have more power to make decisions in their own parliament and assemblies, there will be less power in the Westminster parliament.

   If the other countries can decide how much tax to raise, Westminster will raise less taxes and have less to spend. They may have different priorities, so the countries will become more different.

   > The student is looking at the implications of the change.

   At the moment, there is a point of view in England that MPs from Scotland, Wales and Northern Ireland should not be able to vote at Westminster on issues that only affect England, as English MPs have no say on the decisions made in the other countries.

   > This shows up-to-date knowledge related to the topic.

   As Scotland, Wales and Northern Ireland have the power to make decisions, there may be demand for other regions of the UK to make decisions for themselves. This would reduce the power of Westminster further.

Issues and debates

Source B

Electoral reform: Labour List

In the most disproportionate election result in modern British electoral history, on 7 May 2015, the Conservative Party received 36.9 per cent of the vote and 51 per cent of the seats in Parliament. This caused urgent calls for electoral reform. There is widespread dissatisfaction with first past the post among the public. The Labour Party is especially dissatisfied as it gained votes, but lost seats. A commitment to reform a voting system which clearly does not reflect the preferences of millions of voters would be a wise decision. It would appeal to Green, former Liberal Democrat and especially UKIP voters, all of whose support will be key to winning in 2020.

Source: Adapted from Labour List

Source C

Electoral reform: David Cameron, Conservative Prime Minister

Don't take all this from me. You can judge the relative merits of first past the post and AV, a form of proportional representation, by how popular they are overseas.

Our current system is one of Britain's most successful exports – used by almost half the electors on the planet, embraced and understood by 2.4 billion people from India to America.

So in the next few days ask yourself a few questions: do you want to switch to a voting system that is hopelessly unclear, unfair and indecisive?

Do you want elections that are – as Churchill put it – 'determined by the most worthless votes given for the most worthless candidates'?

And do you want to rip up a valuable part of our constitution and centuries of British history for a system that is unpopular the world over? If the answer is no, make sure you get out to the polling station on 7 May – and vote no to AV.

3. Analyse the sources to identify two views which the writers disagree about. *(2 marks)*

That first past the post is the most popular way of electing people to government.

That first past the post is the fairest way to elect MPs.

4. Which writer do you agree with more? Explain your answer, referring to the arguments made in both sources. *(12 marks)*

I agree that the electoral system should be reformed. The first source shows that the 2015 election was very unfair and the number of votes did not reflect the number of seats that parties won. The Labour Party gained votes but lost seats. The Conservatives won 36.9 per cent of the votes but 51 per cent of the seats in Parliament. Other parties won votes but have very few MPs.

The student is using the material from the source to support their point of view.

Proportional representation means that the number of votes for any party is much closer to the number of seats they end up with in Parliament.

This shows that the student understands how proportional representation works.

David Cameron describes proportional representation as 'hopelessly unclear, unfair and indecisive'. It can take longer to get a result because votes have to be counted several times in order to work out how many MPs each party would have. It doesn't seem unfair to me as the number of votes and seats are much fairer. It can be seen as being indecisive because smaller parties usually get more seats – so there is more likely to be a coalition government. Some people think this is an advantage because it means that large parties have to compromise on their policies.

David Cameron also regards small parties as 'worthless'. In a democracy, everyone is entitled to their opinion – and their vote should count.

Also, just because things have been running for a long time, it doesn't mean that it is right.

There is good evidence in the first source that proportional representation (PR) is a better way of electing people to Parliament. Because first past the post benefits large parties with representation across the country, they are likely to support keeping it because they will not want to give away their advantage.

The student is using their understanding of the concepts to support their point of view and come to a conclusion.

Extended writing

When money is limited, the government must make cuts in all services, however necessary.
How far do you agree with this view?
Give reasons for your opinion, showing that you have considered other points of view.
In your answer, you could consider:
· government spending
· the effect of changes in spending

The government spends a great deal of money every year on a wide range of things we need. This includes health, education, social services, defence and transport as well as looking after the environment and our relations with other countries. There are government departments that run each of these services. The Chancellor of the Exchequer and the Treasury will make the decision about how much is spent on each one.

This shows that the student understands how the system works and who makes the decisions.

Different amounts of money are spent on all these things to meet our needs. The biggest are health, education and social services. The problem about this view is how to decide on what is necessary. Schools and the National Health Service are obviously necessary because people and families need these more at different stages of their lives. People who are old need pensions. Some people in the community need support because they have a disability and are unable to work. We all need a good transport network if we are to get to work or school. Businesses need it too if they are going to get things they make to their destination. There are good reasons not to make any cuts but this is not always possible.

The student raises the key problem here – what is necessary?

Different political parties have different views on what is necessary so the decisions that are made will depend on which party is in power. The Conservative Party tends to think that people should look after themselves. The Labour Party is more prepared to accept responsibility for looking after people who need care.

The student is demonstrating that they understand how different parties are likely to make different decisions.

When making the decisions about how much to spend on each service, a party will think about the effect it will have on voters. Making cuts that affect a party's own supporters is unlikely to be popular – so the Chancellor of the Exchequer will think carefully about such decisions. In a recent budget, the chancellor made cuts that affected the poor and gave tax cuts to the rich. There was a storm of protest and the government had to change its mind.

Good use of a current example as evidence to support the argument.

Now we have fixed terms for elections, it is easier for the government to make such plans as they will know how many more budgets there will be before the election. If governments have to cut spending, they are more likely to do it when the next election is a long way away and to then spend more just before an election, so people feel better off when they come to vote.

This shows a good understanding of the how elections can influence the decisions a government makes.

In my opinion, the government should look at the groups of people who need support the most and make the smallest cuts in the services that they need. Some things can be put off until later when there is more money available.

There are some things, like the money spent on international development, that have been protected. The United Nations set a figure that countries should contribute and the British government has aimed to keep to this. Even when things are difficult here, there are people in other countries who are worse off than us and we should help them.

By looking at spending from this point of view, the government is likely to make fairer decisions.

The student clearly has a good understanding of government spending and this improves the quality of their argument.

How the law works

3.1 What's the point of law?

Getting you thinking

At the beginning of Year 11, Annie, Sanjay, Mikael, Deb, Steve and Al know that they have a hard year ahead if they are to get the GCSEs they want. They are dreaming of the summer when they know it will all be over. The plan is to go on holiday together – somewhere in the sun. It will not be cheap but they are cleaning cars together at the same time as saving up on their own.

1 Why might the friends fall out before July?

2 What rules might they need to set up to stop themselves from falling out?

3 Who sets your school rules?

4 Are people more likely to keep the rules if they have been involved in setting them?

5 What problems would there be if there were no laws?

Why do people obey the law?

Law-abiding citizens obey the law for a variety of reasons: they may have strong religious or moral views about breaking the law; they may be afraid of being caught and arrested; they may fear the shame that going to prison would bring on them and their family; they may be worried about damaging their 'good name' (their reputation).

In some situations it is obvious why a law is needed. If drivers drove through traffic lights on 'stop', they could be seriously injured or killed, or cause injury or death to someone else.

Why do we need laws?

The short answer is, try imagining life without them! Your life would be chaotic, and the most vulnerable members of society, such as the very young, the elderly, the ill and

Breaking the law can damage your good name.

some minorities, would suffer most. What would happen to children, for example, if there were no laws on divorce?

For laws to work properly they need the support of the majority of the population. Most people agree that child abuse is a shocking crime and abusers must be punished. But public opinion is more divided on euthanasia. Some think it wrong to treat doctors as criminals if they help terminally ill patients in pain to die. Others would argue that this is morally wrong as well as unlawful.

Who's the loser?

A shoplifter who has stolen a couple of T-shirts might argue that their actions won't put a big company like Marks and Spencer out of business. But:

- if everybody stole from them it would push up prices for everyone else who shops there, because Marks and Spencer would have to pay for the T-shirts

- if you steal from Marks and Spencer, you steal from the people who own the business, so it's just like stealing a mobile phone or a car.

In the same way, if people don't pay income tax when they should, the government will have less money to pay for schools and hospitals. Many people are therefore affected indirectly by tax evasion.

Some of your **legal rights** in the UK

Age

10	13	16	17	18
Criminal responsibilty	Get a part-time job	Get married Leave school Work full time Buy a lottery ticket Join the armed forces	Drive car Pilot a plane	Vote in an election Make a will Buy fireworks

1 Why does the law impose age limits like these?

2 Which of these age limits would you change? Explain why.

3 Whose human rights are being protected by each of these age limits?

Why do laws change?

There are laws to cover a vast range of activities, including adoption, marriage and divorce, terrorism, discrimination, motoring, banking, sex, drugs, theft and assault. Laws change for all sorts of reasons, including scientific and technological developments. The internet and cloning, for example, led to changes.

Our changing values also mean that laws have to change. We now have laws about discrimination which mean that people cannot be treated differently. These have been introduced as our values have changed.

Action

1 In groups, think about your usual daily routine and list how many times during the day you come across a rule or law. Why do you choose to obey or not to obey these rules and laws?

2 You sometimes hear people say 'But it's a bad law.' Make a list of your reasons for laws being good or bad. Be ready to explain your ideas.

Check your understanding

1 In your own words, give four reasons why people obey the law. Suggest one more reason not mentioned on these pages.

2 Make a list of crimes that have immediate consequences for the general public. List others that may have long-term and less immediate consequences.

3 Why do you think it is important that the majority of citizens support a particular law?

Another point of view

'You should never break the law.'

Key terms

legal right: a right that is protected by law

3.2 What is law?

Getting you thinking

On Christmas Day, the body of a girl was found in the countryside. She was just 25 and had enjoyed a night out with friends before she disappeared. The police set up a widespread search for clues and a suspect. They arrested her landlord, who had a flat in the building where she lived. He protested his innocence and was eventually released. He was under arrest but had not been charged when the newspapers printed stories that assumed he was guilty. Headlines like these ran thoughout the tabloid press.

He defended himself to the media. 'I did not kill her,' said another headline.

On 20 January another of her neighbours was arrested and later found guilty.

Weird, posh, lewd and creepy

Suspect – a peeping Tom

1 What was wrong with the action of the media?

2 If the landlord had been charged, how might the reporting of the crime have affected the outcome of a trial?

3 How do you think individuals should be protected by the law?

Law protects our rights and freedoms

In the UK our lives are ruled by laws. In other societies, people's lives might be under the control of kings, presidents or others who have the right to rule. The law in the UK also applies to the lawmakers – so everyone must abide by the law. This is known as the **rule of law**. There are some principles that affect the way in which laws are applied.

- **Innocent until proved guilty**
  Anyone who is brought to court is said to be innocent until they are proved guilty. This means that the court must present evidence to prove that a person is guilty beyond reasonable doubt.

- **Equality before the law**
  The law applies to everyone equally, whatever their gender, ethnicity, religion, age or disability.

- **Access to justice**
  Everyone has the right to use the legal system whether they have been charged with an offence or have been hurt in some way. Today, in the UK, the cost might limit access to the legal system.

The person in court is innocent until proved guilty.

You will find out how the law protects our rights and freedom.

Where does our law come from?

The main source of law in the UK is legislation. This includes all laws passed by Parliament – as you discovered on page 66.

The other sources of law are:

- Common law – this is made by judges who make decisions which must be followed by all other courts. This is known as **case law or precedent**. One example of this was the decision that someone who is accused of murder cannot use the fact that they were threatened as a defence.

- European Union law – as the UK is a member of the European Union (EU), UK law must conform to EU law.

The UK is a member of the Council of Europe and has signed up to the European Convention on Human Rights, which you found at about on page 31. The UK's Human Rights Act means that the courts in the UK must protect the rights identified in the ECHR.

The law across the UK

There are different systems of justice in England and Wales, Scotland and Northern Ireland. You found out about the parliaments and assemblies of the different countries of the UK on page 68.

England and Wales have the same legal system, and laws passed by the UK Parliament automatically apply to Wales. The Welsh Assembly has passed some laws which apply only to Wales but, as yet, there are no major differences between the two countries.

Scotland has its own system of laws and courts, and its own Parliament.

Northern Ireland has a similar system to that of England and Wales.

Judges can make law.

Check your understanding

1 What does the rule of law mean?

2 Explain the principles that affect how the law is applied.

3 Most of our laws are made in Parliament. Explain other ways laws are made.

4 Is law the same throughout the UK?

Another point of view

'The UK should be able to ignore the European Convention on Human Rights when it makes laws.'

Key terms

case law or precedent: once a decision has been made in a court it becomes law in all future cases containing the same material facts and it must be followed by all lower courts

rule of law: a country is governed by law and all residents must obey the law – so no one is above the law

Getting you thinking

Biker's murderers jailed for life

1 Which case is a private issue?

2 Which case involved the police?

3 Which case is more worrying for the general public? Why?

4 Can you think of some other examples of private issues and of some which involve the police?

Facebook libel

Sharon Smith, a fitness instructor, fell out with her friend Joanne Walder. She posted an untrue message about Joanne on her Facebook wall. She had intended to send the message to one of her friends but it went to all 300. Her sister then re-posted it to all of her 650 connections.

Joanne sued Sharon for libel and the High Court decided that her reputation had been damaged.

Two kinds of law

Over many centuries of law making, two separate but related branches of the law have evolved to meet changing circumstances: **civil law** and **criminal law**.

Most civil cases are about disputes between individuals or groups, and very often these arguments are about rights. Examples include company law, adoption, accidents at work and consumer rights.

Criminal law deals with offences such as murder, theft and drug dealing. In a criminal case, the conflict is between the government (acting for all citizens) and the lawbreakers.

Who's right?

The person who brings a case to a civil court is called the claimant. The person accused of doing wrong is called the defendant. In some civil cases, the claimant sets out to **sue** the defendant. If the claimant wins, the defendant will have to give the claimant money, which is known as damages.

JK Rowling sued the *Daily Mail* for claiming that she had written a sob story about her life as a single mum. The judge decided that the paper's story wasn't accurate and that JK Rowling should be awarded damages. The *Daily Mail* apologised and paid the damages. The amount was kept private. JK Rowling donated the damages to charity.

A civil court

A **judge** sitting without a jury decides almost all civil cases.

Criminal courts

There is a separate system of courts to deal with criminal cases. Less serious offences are dealt with in **magistrates' courts**. Serious offences are dealt with in **crown courts** before a judge and a **jury**.

Another point of view

'Neighbours should sort things out instead of going to court.'

What happens in a civil court?

Most civil cases are heard in a **county court**. Because a court case can be very expensive, most people try to settle the dispute before it gets to court.

A small number of civil cases are heard in a **High Court**. These courts deal with complex family disputes and other complicated financial and legal matters, such as bankruptcy and large claims for damages. Any case involving £50 000 or more is heard in the High Court.

If a civil case involves a claim of less than £10 000, it will be heard in a **small claims court**. About 90 000 cases a year are heard in these courts.

Action

Make a list of the different kind of cases that appear in civil courts. Which human rights are involved in each type?

Check your understanding

1 What are the main differences between civil and criminal cases?

2 What is a) a claimant, b) a defendant and c) a small claims court?

3 What type of crime is dealt with in either magistrates' courts or crown courts?

4 Why are most civil cases settled before they reach court?

Key terms

civil law: this covers disputes between individuals or groups. Civil law cases are often about rights

county court: a local court that has limited powers in civil cases

criminal law: this deals with offences such as murder and drug dealing. These cases are between the Crown Prosecution Service (acting for all citizens) and the offender

crown court: courts held in towns in England and Wales where judges hear criminal cases

High Court: the court where judges hear cases on serious crimes

judge: a person who decides questions of law in a court

jury: a group of people who decide if someone is guilty in a court of law

magistrates' court: a court held before two or more public officers dealing with minor crimes

small claims court: a local court, which hears civil cases involving small amounts of money

sue: to make a claim against someone or something

3.4 Who puts the law into practice?

Getting you thinking

1 You've broken the law and have to appear in court. Which of the following would you prefer as your 'judge and jury', and why:

- your teachers
- your classmates
- your parents
- the police
- other young people who've been in trouble themselves
- the victims of your crime
- a group of people chosen at random, who do not know you?

2 Which group do you think the victim would prefer? Give reasons.

3 Which group do you think would give the fairest outcome? Give reasons.

The criminal justice system

The criminal justice system is large and complex. These are the roles within it.

Judges

The judges who work in both criminal and civil courts are known collectively as the **judiciary**. Most judges have worked for at least 10 years as a barrister, but a few solicitors also become judges. In a jury trial, it is the jury that decides if the accused is guilty or not, but the judge who determines the sentence.

Senior judges (who sit in the higher courts) are very powerful. They don't make laws; Parliament does that. You found out about how laws are made on page 66, but if there is an argument about how a law should be interpreted, it is the senior judges who decide.

Magistrates

Full-time magistrates are called district judges and are paid for their work. They are usually barristers or solicitors with at least seven years' experience. They sit alone.

Part-time magistrates come from all walks of life. They are not legally qualified and are not paid. They work with other magistrates.

Jury

A jury is made up of 12 adults, who sit in a crown court and decide whether the accused person is innocent or guilty. A jury is made up of members of the public chosen at random.

Police

The police do not make laws; they enforce them. Their job is to protect the public, arrest lawbreakers and bring them before the courts.

The Crown Prosecution Service (CPS)

The CPS advises the police on cases for possible prosecution. It reviews cases submitted by the police for prosecution and, when the decision is made to prosecute, it decides the charge in the more serious and complex cases. The CPS also prepares cases for court and presents them at court.

Solicitors

All **solicitors** must pass law exams because, among other things, they can give legal advice to people who have to go to court. Some solicitors also speak in court on behalf of their clients.

Barristers

Barristers undergo a long legal training too, but they spend most of their time in court representing their clients. They are the only lawyers qualified to speak in all types of court.

Probation officers

If an offender is given a community sentence, they will work with a local **probation officer**. Probation officers are professionally qualified. They write court reports on offenders and supervise them in the community when they've been sentenced.

A new uniform has been designed for judges in civil cases. It aims to make them less remote from the public. Do you think it works? If so, explain why.

Action

1 Research the entry requirements (that is, age, qualifications, etc.) of either a police officer or a solicitor.

2 Interview a probation officer to find out about the work they do with offenders in the community. You may wish to research a specific aspect of their work. For example, probation officers often work with young offenders who have problems with alcohol and other drugs.

3 Research who can be called for jury service and what serving on a jury involves.

Check your understanding

1 What do judges do in trials where there is a jury?

2 What powers do senior judges have?

3 What is the most important difference between the role of the police and the role of judges?

4 What is the difference between a barrister and a solicitor?

5 What skills and personal qualities do you think you need to be a good magistrate?

6 Can you think of any reasons why people don't apply to be magistrates?

Key terms

barrister: a lawyer who represents and speaks for their clients in court

judiciary: all the judges in a country

probation officer: someone who writes court reports on offenders and supervises them in the community

solicitor: a lawyer who gives legal advice and may speak for their clients in court

3.5 Criminal courts

Getting you thinking

1 Which of the two courtrooms above is the most 'child friendly' and why?

2 Should courts be made more 'adult friendly'? Give reasons.

3 Is it a good idea that courts are open to the public? Give reasons.

4 The results of court cases are published in newspapers. What effect might this have on people who think about committing a crime?

Two types of court

Courts are formal places. Everyone involved must take the process very seriously. In some countries, youth courts are more informal because people think young people are more likely to tell the truth in a more relaxed environment.

There are two types of court for criminal cases: magistrates' courts and crown courts.

A magistrates' court

Over 95 per cent of all criminal trials take place in magistrates' courts. Specially trained magistrates also run youth courts for offenders aged between 10 and 17. Magistrates, who sit in court with at least one other magistrate, also deal with a small number of civil cases.

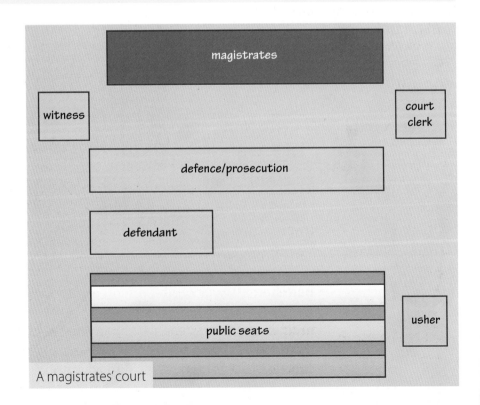

A magistrates' court

Mitigating factors

There is no jury in a magistrates' court, so magistrates must be absolutely sure 'beyond reasonable doubt' that the accused person (the defendant) is guilty. They must also take into account any **mitigating factors**. If, for example, a woman stole from a supermarket because she had no money to buy food for herself and her children, magistrates would take this into account and might give her a lesser sentence.

What sentences can magistrates give?

Magistrates have the power to give the following penalties:

- prison: up to a maximum of six months
- community sentences
- Antisocial Behaviour Orders (ASBOs)
- Criminal Behaviour Orders (CBOs)
- fines
- discharge: conditional or absolute.

A crown court

The most serious criminal cases are heard in a crown court. The atmosphere is more solemn and the proceedings are more formal than in a magistrates' court. The judges and barristers wear wigs and gowns. A jury decides if the defendant is guilty or not (unless the defendant pleads guilty, in which case no jury is involved).

Crown court judges can have different powers. Only High Court judges, who sit in the larger courts, can try very serious cases, such as murder and rape. Others, known as circuit judges and **recorders**, try less serious cases, such as theft.

Crown court judges and juries must also take into account any mitigating factors, in the same way that magistrates do. The maximum sentence in a crown court is life imprisonment.

A crown court

Check your understanding

1 What are 'mitigating factors'? Support your answer with an example.
2 What kinds of mitigating factors might influence magistrates' decisions when sentencing young offenders?
3 List the differences between a magistrates' court and a crown court.
4 What is the maximum sentence each type of court can impose?
5 When is a jury used in a crown court case?

Another point of view

'Courts should be friendlier places.'

Key terms

mitigating factors: reasons why an offender might be given a lighter sentence
recorder: a barrister or solicitor of at least 10 years' experience, who acts as a part-time judge in a crown court

3.6 Solving civil disputes

Getting you thinking

Shut that gate!

Two couples shared a drive to their houses in Formby, Lancashire. The Heslins wanted the gates left open. The Bradleys wanted them shut.

At one point, the Bradleys padlocked the gates to stop the Heslins getting in or out at all.

The Heslins offered to install electronic gates, but this was ignored.

After two years of fighting, the row ended up in the High Court. The judge decided that while the Bradleys were entitled to close their gates, they must not do so at times which 'substantially interfere' with the Heslins' enjoyment of their home.

The two couples ended up paying over £100 000 to cover the costs of the dispute.

1 What are the drawbacks to taking a dispute like this to court?

2 Who wins from such disputes?

3 Can you suggest other ways in which such problems might be resolved?

4 Apart from money, what are the advantages of settling disputes without going to court?

Is there another way?

Civil courts have been the standard way of solving disputes but, as the story of the gates suggest, it is often not the best solution. Some problems are dealt with by tribunals and others might go through the small claims court. You found out about the small claims court on page 85.

Tribunals are often used to resolve work-based problems, although there are tribunals in many other fields, such as asylum and mental health issues. They are less formal than courts but produce rulings that are legally binding. An expert judge takes the lead with experts who understand the issues.

There are also ways to avoid the legal system all together. These include mediation or arbitration.

Ombudsmen

Many government agencies and professional organisations have an **ombudsman**, who makes decisions when people think they have been treated badly. If you think a bank has behaved badly, you would go the financial ombudsman. Ombudsmen also work in the fields of property, housing, the law, local government, and the prison and probation services, among others.

Ombudsmen are independent, free of charge and unbiased – they don't take sides with either the person who is complaining or the organisation being complained about.

You usually have to go through the organisation's complaints procedure before going to the ombudsman, so it can take a long time. If an ombudsman finds that your complaint is justified, they will recommend what should be done to put things right. An ombudsman can't force an organisation to go along with the recommendations, but they almost always do.

Mediation

Mediation can be used to resolve all sorts of disputes, including housing, families, employment, consumer issues and problems between neighbours.

- **What are the advantages?**

- **How does it work?**
A **mediator**, who doesn't take one side or the other, helps both sides to work out the problem and attempt to come to some agreement. If discussions are successful, both sides can sign a legally binding agreement. If they can't agree, they can still go to court.

Mediation is much cheaper than going to court.

It is not adversarial as it tries to get people to agree.

It is more flexible and informal.

It can be quicker than court.

The solution may be longlasting.

There are more solutions. You might just want an apology, for example.

Here are some examples of costs for online mediation through the government's Department of Justice.

Amount you are claiming	Fees for each side	Length of session
£5000 or less	£50 + VAT £100 + VAT	1 hour 2 hours
£5000 to £15 000	£300 + VAT	3 hours
£15 000 to £50 000	£425 + VAT	4 hours

Check your understanding

1 What sort of claims does the small claims court deal with?

2 What sort of issues can be taken to a tribunal?

3 Who makes the judgments in a tribunal?

4 What does a mediator do?

5 How might a mediator have helped the Bradleys and Heslins?

6 What advantages does mediation have over going to court?

7 Give one advantage and one disadvantage of going to an ombudsman.

Another point of view

'Going to court is an expensive waste of time.'

Key terms

mediator: acting as a go-between between people in dispute in order to resolve the problem

ombudsman: an official who is appointed to investigate individuals' complaints against a company or an organisation

tribunals: these are set up to resolve certain types of dispute, such as employment issues

3.7 What sort of sentence?

Getting you thinking

Mrs B stole £500.

Mr G stole £50.

Look at the list of possible decisions below. Which would be the fairest? Give reasons.

a) Both Mrs B and Mr G should get the same sentence.

b) Mrs B should get a tougher sentence because she stole more.

c) Mrs B should get a lighter sentence because she's old and poor.

d) Mrs B should get a lighter sentence because she's a woman.

What's the purpose of punishment?

Judges and magistrates have reasons for deciding on the sentence of an offender. Their motives will be a combination of the following objectives:

- to punish the offender
- to protect the public
- to change the offender's behaviour
- to ensure that the offender does something to make up for their crime
- to reduce crime in the future.

Different people have different views on which are most important. Most judges or magistrates will want to try to ensure that the offender does not get into trouble again.

What's the sentence?

There is a range of punishments that may be given to an offender. If a defendant pleads guilty or gives evidence against another defendant, the sentences might be reduced. This is called plea bargaining.

A discharge

An offender is given a **discharge** if they are guilty of a minor crime and the decision is not to punish them at this time. An absolute discharge means that no action will be taken. A conditional discharge means that the offender won't be punished unless they commit another offence within a set period of time.

A fine

Fines are the most common criminal sentence. They're usually given for less serious crimes such as driving offences, minor theft or criminal damage. The amount of the fine depends on the seriousness of the crime and the offender's ability to pay.

Community sentence

Community sentences set out the conditions that an offender must fulfil over a period of time. The objective is both to punish them and reduce the risk of them offending again.

Usually offenders are given a period of Community Payback, which means they have to do unpaid work to repay their neighbourhood for their crimes. It can range from 40 to 300 hours' work.

Many offenders have problems of various sorts, so they are told to carry out some of the following to help them in the future:

- get training so they can find a job
- have treatment for any conditions they have, such as drug or alcohol addiction
- not go to places where they are likely to get into trouble
- obey a curfew which limits when they can go out and wear an electronic tag
- live at a particular place
- meet a probation officer regularly to check their progress
- take part in group activities at an attendance centre to help them live responsibly in the community.

Restorative justice can be used to bring offenders together with their victims to help them to understand the effect of their actions.

Prison sentence

A prison sentence will be given when the court believes the public must be protected from the offender.

Offenders can be given a determinate sentence or indeterminate sentence. A determinate sentence means that they serve a fixed length of time, such as five years. Half of it will be served in prison and the rest in the community. They will be on licence and the probation service will supervise them.

An indeterminate sentence has no fixed end point. It is usually given to people who are a threat to society and will not be let out until they are thought to be safe.

Suspended sentence

A first-time offender may get a suspended sentence. This means they will not go to prison if they do not reoffend and if they follow orders in much the same way as those with a community sentence. If they break the rules, they will usually be sent to prison.

Deciding on the sentence

The decision made by magistrates and judges when they find someone guilty of a crime depends upon:

- the type of crime and how serious it is
- the law and sentencing guidelines
- if the offender admits their guilt
- the offender's criminal history
- the offender's personal and financial circumstances.

They will weigh up the situation for each individual and consider any mitigating factors. For example, a young man who has had a difficult family life, has not done well in education and has had trouble getting a job might not be sent to prison but might instead be given a community sentence to help him get back on track.

Check your understanding

1 What does punishment aim to achieve?
2 Why are people given different sorts of sentence?
3 What are the judges and magistrates trying to achieve with the different sentences?
4 What is mitigation? Give some examples.

Action

Use this website to help you understand how sentences are worked out in different situations: http://ybtj.justice.gov.uk.

Another point of view

'Giving someone a community service means just letting them off.'

Key terms

community sentence: a sentence which allows people to continue to live in the community under certain conditions

discharge: not being sentenced for a minor crime; it can be conditional

restorative justice: a system of criminal justice which aims to rehabilitate offenders through meeting and talking to victims and the community

Getting you thinking

In reception at the Youth Offending Service I saw Ed again. We always set each other off – and when he shoved me I thumped him and we both ended up brawling on the floor. The staff did their best to keep us apart, but we were always bumping into each other, even in court, and it usually ended in trouble.

When they suggested mediation, I told them what I thought, but in the end they persuaded me to give it a go. We had some meetings – just me and then with my parents. Then we all met together. By the end we had agreed not to fight any more. It was really hard. At later meetings we tried to work out why we'd got like this. I got quite upset when we talked it out, but now we can just say 'Hi' and ignore the others who bait us to fight.

1 Why do you think the two boys were always fighting?

2 They have been in court for getting into trouble. What sort of sentence might they have been given?

3 How do you think mediation helped them?

4 What do you think might have happened to them without mediation?

Who are the young offenders?

Many young people who end up in court come from troubled backgrounds or have difficulty with education for a variety of reasons. The number who appear in court has fallen steadily, but the group who end up in custody are very likely to reoffend.

The aim of the **youth justice system** is to try to prevent young people from ending up in trouble, but it doesn't always succeed. It is important to try to keep young people out of prison as they are much more likely to reoffend.

Dealing with young offenders

The criminal law and the UK court system realise that young people, between the ages of 10 and 17, should be treated differently from adults.

Arrest

If you are arrested before you are 18, the police must try to contact your parent, guardian or carer. You cannot be questioned without having an 'appropriate adult' with you. This includes a parent, guardian, carer, social worker, family member, friend or volunteer who is over 18.

Cautions

If you commit an offence which is not serious enough for trial, you will receive a caution. The Youth Offending Team will assess your needs and decide on a programme of rehabilitation and education. The team is made up of people from the police, probation, health, education and children's services.

Youth court

If the offence is serious, you will be sent for trial in a **youth court**. You will be referred to the Youth Offending Team. The team will go on working with you when you are sentenced.

A youth court differs from adult courts.

- There is no jury.

- The public is not allowed in.

- A parent or guardian must be there.

- Offenders are called by their first name.

If the offence is very serious, such as rape or murder, a **young offender's** trial would begin in the in a youth court, but the case would be tried in a crown court.

Sentences for young offenders

Discharge – either absolute or with conditions.

Custodial sentence – a young offender aged from 12 to 17 years may receive a Detention and Training Order lasting between 4 months and 2 years.

Fines – if under 16, parents pay the fine.

For the most serious offences – the young offender receives long-term detention of up to 14 years, and for murder can be sentenced to 'detention during Her Majesty's pleasure', which means a minimum of 12 years.

Referral orders – the young offender attend a youth offender panel to agree a contract for three months or up to a year. The young offender agrees to abide by certain rules to avoid more serious punishment. This may involve restorative justice.

Under 10 – a Local Child Curfew will be imposed, which means the offender must be at home between 9 p.m. and 6 a.m. unless with an adult. They will be referred to the Youth Offending Team.

Youth rehabilitation orders – the young offender commits to rehabilitation for up to three years. The conditions can included a curfew, unpaid work, drug rehabilitation and education.

Check your understanding

1 What is happening to the number of young people who appear in court?

2 What is the aim of the youth justice system?

3 Why is it important to keep young people out of prison?

4 How is the youth justice system different from the adult system? Why?

5 What sentences can be given to young people?

Another point of view

'Young people should be treated harshly to prevent them reoffending.'

Key terms

youth court: a court that deals with young offenders
youth justice system: the part of the justice system that deals with young people
young offenders: offenders between the ages of 10 and 17

3.9 What's happening to crime?

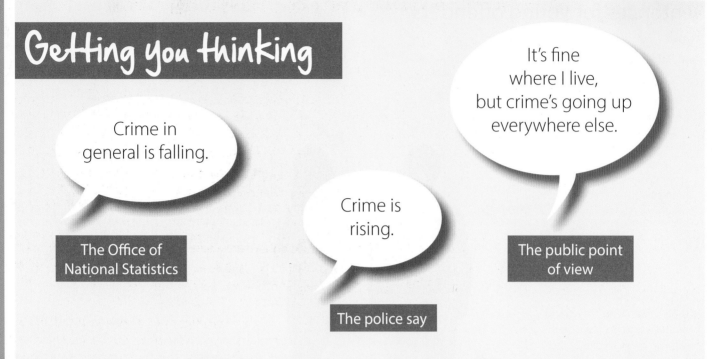

Getting you thinking

Crime in general is falling.

The Office of National Statistics

Crime is rising.

The police say

It's fine where I live, but crime's going up everywhere else.

The public point of view

1 Why do you think people think crime is worse in places where they don't live?

2 Why do you think counting crimes might be difficult?

3 What advice would you give if you were in charge of counting crime?

Why do people commit crimes?

There are many views on why people commit crimes. It is thought that when there is greater inequality in income and education people are more likely to commit crimes.

Drugs and alcohol also affect the way people behave. Although the amount of alcohol-related crime has been falling over past years, many victims of violent crime still think that their attacker was under the influence of alcohol.

The environment can affect how people behave. In streets that are dirty, full of rubbish and graffiti, there is likely to be more crime.

Why do people reoffend?

Once people have been in trouble with the police, they are much more likely to **reoffend**, particularly if they have been in prison.

- 47 per cent of people leaving prison reoffend within a year.

- 58 per cent of people on short sentences reoffend in a year.

- 70 per cent of under 18s leaving prison reoffend in a year.

People in prison often lose contact with their families. They generally have poor education or mental health problems and therefore have difficulty fitting back into everyday life. People on short sentences get less help to put their lives back on track when they are in prison because there isn't time.

There is a growing view that prisoners should be given more responsibility to help them deal with the world outside prison.

You will find out about the changes that are taking place in crime rates.

3.9 What's happening to crime?

Prison Radio

National Prison Radio broadcasts to prisons across England and Wales. It is run by the Prison Radio Association charity whose staff work alongside prisoners – together they have produced many award-winning programmes.

'Reducing reoffending is of benefit to everybody. Equipping prisoners with skills and confidence is crucial in bringing down reoffending rates. Prison radio offers a unique, innovative and effective way to communicate with prisoners and engage them in education, debate and community.'

What do the numbers say?

The Crime Survey for England and Wales shows a steady decline in violent crime over the last 20 years.

- Violent crime rates have fallen by more than half since peaking in the mid-1990s.
- Homicide has shown a general downward trend since 2002/03.
- In 2015, the number of sexual offences was the highest recorded by the police since 2002/03.
- There was a 5 per cent decrease in gun crime in one year.
- Offences involving knives or sharp instruments fell by 2 per cent in one year.

In 2015, total crime rose because cybercrime was included for the first time. The data is affected by such changes almost every year.

Are the figures accurate?

The **Office for National Statistics** records crime falling, but the police say it's rising. Who's right?

The evidence

- There is evidence which says that fewer people have been treated in hospital for injuries resulting from violent crime.
- Homicide is unlikely to be under-reported. Murders are currently shown to be lower than in 1977.
- Sexual offences have probably been under-reported in the past, but people are now more willing to come forward.
- The Crime Survey of England and Wales does not collect data on crimes against businesses.
- The police used to under-record crime because it made them look better and there was uncertainly about what they should record. They have been told to improve the way they record crimes – so the figures have risen. This was particularly true of sexual offences.
- It would seem that crime is falling and the police data is catching up and being recorded more accurately.

Check your understanding

1 Why do people commit crimes? Can you suggest any other reasons, apart from those listed?
2 What do the official crime statistics tell us?
3 What problems are there in collecting data about crime?
4 What sort of evidence can be used to show that violent crime is falling?
5 Why do you think people think crime is rising?
6 What sort of crime do you think is rising?

Action

Go to this website to check crime statistics in your area. Compare it with another area.
http://www.crime-statistics.co.uk/postcode

Another point of view

'If crime is falling, the government doesn't need to spend so much money on policing.'

Key terms

Office for National Statistics: the organisation that collects data about what is happening in the UK

reoffend: to commit a crime more than once

Getting you thinking

Annie Lewis, mum of three and local businesswoman, runs her local **Neighbourhood Watch** scheme.

'I want to participate in order to generate awareness of community safety in the area where we live. I want to make the area round my home a happy and a safe place to live.'

'If you want to live in a community where we can help each other, communicate, look out for each other and care for the place we live in, then join this scheme. Homeowners and tenants in the area who wish to join a lively and informative scheme are all invited. Not formal, just organised, friendly and kind!'

1 How does a Neighbourhood Watch scheme help to reduce crime?

2 Why is it good for people who live in the area?

3 Are there other reasons why it might help a community?

4 How might it help the individual who runs a scheme?

Reducing crime in your community

Neighbourhood Watch is just one example of community activities to reduce crime in local areas. It offers a mix of prevention and protection. There are other examples from across the country.

Merton & Sutton Mediation helps to resolve neighbourhood disputes.

Tomorrow's Women Wirral in Cheshire provides courses and support for women with drug and alcohol problems.

Community Triggers allow people who have been affected by antisocial behaviour to call for a review with all the organisations that are involved in the problem.

Eastbourne Neighbourhood Panels bring together local residents and the Neighbourhood Policing Team to discuss issues and work out how to prevent crime.

Methods of preventing crime

There is some debate about the best way to deal with crime and criminals. Some people want to lock people up and throw away the key, but others look for effective ways of preventing people reoffending or getting involved in the first place. Here are some ways to prevent crime happening.

Supporting children

People who commit crimes often have deprived family backgrounds and poor education. There is a strong link between children who have experienced abuse and neglect and future crime, so support for families and schools in deprived neighbourhoods is important in preventing crime in the future.

Reducing opportunities

By improving the environment, opportunities for crime can be be reduced. Better lighting on streets and in hidden corners of shopping centres or housing all help.

By reducing access to drugs, alcohol and weapons, people are less likely to have the opportunity or desire to commit crimes.

Distracting young people by engaging them in enjoyable activities – perhaps with cash-back schemes to reward those who change their habits – may deter them from committing crimes.

You will find out how to reduce crime through prevention, protection or punishment.

Improving the environment can reduce the level of crime.

Deterring offenders

Reducing the chance of people getting away with their crimes is a strong deterrent. This can be done by having more police and community schemes. By developing a stronger trust in our legal system – or the rule of law – and concern for communities, fewer people are likely to offend.

Reduce the risk of reoffending

Keeping people in touch with their families when they are in prison and helping them to find work when they leave both help people not to reoffend. **Rehabilitation programmes** while they are in prison also help.

Since many prisoners suffer from drink and drugs problems, it is important to give them proper support.

If all else fails…

People often assume that the death penalty will reduce crime, but research in the USA shows that murder is as common in states with the death penalty as in those without it.

Prison does protect people from crime, but it also makes people more likely to reoffend – especially young people and adults with short sentences.

Suspended sentences work well because offenders are told that if they offend again in a given time period, they will go to prison. Community sentences are also effective because people continue to live in the community and can be given training or rehabilitation to help them sort out their lives. These sentences are considered by some people to be a soft option, but they are much more successful at reducing reoffending.

Fines are less effective than suspended sentences and community orders, probably because they are a one-off payment without any follow-up.

Check your understanding

1 How can communities help reduce crime?
2 How do strategies to reduce crime help?
3 What is the effect of different sorts of punishment?

Another point of view

'Every offender should be given a community sentence.'

Key terms

Neighbourhood Watch: a scheme in which members of the community take responsibility for keeping an eye on each other's property to prevent crime
rehabilitation programmes: programmes which help people to overcome problems so they can avoid committing crimes in future

Getting you thinking

Besnik Vrapi was a student at the University of East London. He signed up to be a special constable, a volunteer with the police force, because he thought it would be interesting thing to do in his spare time.

Soon after his training, he found himself in the middle of the London riots. He remembers being sent to talk to a bunch of young guys who were looking for trouble. 'I just tried to stay calm. I told them it wasn't fair to damage other people's homes and businesses and that they should go home. They listened to me, and in the end they left. I realised this is a job where you really can make a difference.'

1 What is a special constable?

2 How did Besnik make a difference?

3 Why do people want to make a difference?

4 Can you think of any other benefits of being a special constable?

Taking part in the legal system

Many people in the UK take a role in the running of the legal system. It may be voluntary, compulsory, paid or unpaid – but whatever the job, they are supporting their community.

Jury service

If you are called for jury service, it is compulsory to attend. Under special circumstances, you may be allowed to postpone for a short period of time. Usually, the court you are asked to attend will be close to your home.

As a member of a jury, you must not discuss the trial with anyone or research the crime on the internet. This is to prevent you being influenced by others when you are asked to make a decision about whether the defendant is innocent or guilty.

Becoming a magistrate

Magistrates hear cases in courts in their community. They usually sit with two other magistrates and together they decide whether a defendant is innocent or guilty. Once the decision is made, they will decide on the sentence. Very serious crimes are sent to a higher court.

Most people between the ages off 18 and 65 can apply to be a magistrate. Applicants are given training in how to carry out the role. They do not need to have a legal background, as court officials will give them advice.

You will find out about your rights and how you can contribute to the legal system.

3.11 The law: a citizen's responsibilities and rights

Your rights

Your rights as a citizen were explained on page 34.

If you are **arrested**, however, you will be taken to a police station and put in a cell. Whatever you have done, you still have certain rights.

You must be

- told the reason for your arrest
- given the opportunity to tell someone about your arrest
- able to get free legal advice from a solicitor
- offered medical help if you are feeling ill
- able to see a written notice about your rights (e.g. to regular breaks for food and to use the toilet).

You can ask to see the notice in your language or for an interpreter to explain it to you.

Becoming a special constable

Special constables are trained volunteers who work with and support their local police. All sorts of people become 'specials', as special constables are known. They may be teachers, taxi drivers or accountants or have any number of other careers. They all volunteer to work with the full-time police for a minimum of four hours a week. They form a vital link between the regular police and the local community.

Once their training is completed, they have the same powers as regular officers and wear a similar uniform.

Being a member of a tribunal hearing

Tribunals are specialist courts which decide disputes in specific areas of law. They hear about a million cases each year. This is more than any other part of the justice system.

Tribunals decide a wide range of cases, including workplace disputes, the licensing of gang masters and criminal injuries compensation. They also deal with appeals against decisions of government departments, such as social security benefits and immigration and asylum.

A tribunal is headed by a judge, who sits with people who are experts in the field. They might be doctors, accountants or surveyors, for example, depending on the subject of the hearing. They provide a practical, specialist view of the facts and evidence before the tribunal and take an equal part in the decision made by the tribunal.

Action

Find out what happens to a juror who breaks the rules.

Check your understanding

1 Is jury service voluntary?
2 Why is it important not to discuss the trial if you are on a jury?
3 Do magistrates need a legal background?
4 Can magistrates judge very serious crimes?
5 How many hours must a special constable work?
6 Do specials have the same powers as full-time police officers?
7 What is a tribunal?
8 What is the role of a tribunal member?
9 What are your rights on arrest?

Another point of view

'Citizens must play their part in the legal system, not just leave it to the experts.'

Key terms

arrested: a person who is arrested is held against their will because they are suspected of committing a crime

special constable: a volunteer police officer

3.12 Bringing it all together

Source A

Changes in youth justice

Lord McNally, chair of the Youth Justice Board, said that the combined efforts of the YJB and the youth justice system to divert children and young people from crime and address the causes of their offending behaviour have resulted in the number of first-time entrants to the system dropping dramatically in recent years.

'Those that remain in the system have complex needs and are, on balance, more challenging to work with,' he said.

'This means that it is important for the system to meet their needs to stop them reoffending.'

'I particularly welcome the recommendation that legal practitioners who represent children and young people should receive appropriate training, and agree that the closer involvement of children's services with looked-after children in the youth justice system, particularly at court, is to be encouraged.'

Source: Children & Young People Now

1. Suggest two reasons why the number of 'first-time entrants' to the youth justice system is falling. *(2 marks)*

    Young people are committing fewer crimes.

    The youth justice system is using other methods to try to prevent them committing crimes.

2. Give two different punishments that a young offender might receive. *(2 marks)*

    Referral orders and youth rehabilitation orders.

    > There are also the usual punishments that apply to adults. These would earn marks too.

3. The source looks at changes in youth justice. Explain, with reference to the source, how and why young people should be treated differently by the courts. *(6 marks)*

    Young people who appear in court should be treated differently because courts are frightening places and it can be hard to understand what is going on.

    Many young people who commit crimes have complex needs and therefore the court should try to take the problems into account in order to try to prevent them reoffending. Young people who are sent to prison are very likely to reoffend so it is important to find different ways of dealing with them, such as referral orders and youth rehabilitation orders.

    Children's services are often involved and this helps looked-after children who do not have families to support them. It also brings together all the people who are concerned about the child's future and keeping them out of trouble in future.

Issues and debates

Source B

Prisons and public opinion

Lord Ashcroft carried out a survey into crime and public opinion. Here are some of the views people expressed.

They thought that sentencing for convicted criminals in Britain is too soft. There were several elements to this: they thought that if offenders went to prison at all their sentence would be too short; they would then serve only half the time they were sentenced to because of the cost or lack of space; and the time they did spend inside would be much too comfortable to constitute a proper punishment or a deterrent to reoffending.

'It's really cushy. They have TVs in their rooms, PlayStations, a pool table, a big social room where they go and sit. Life in prison is better than life outside.'

Source: Crime, Punishment & The People, Lord Ashcroft.

Source C

The Justice Secretary speaks about prisons

Michael Gove, the Justice Secretary, spoke to the Howard League for Penal Reform. He wants to see change in our prisons and the way people are sentenced. Here are some of the views he expressed.

He wants to reduce prison numbers in England and Wales, and believes it will fall over time.

Rehabilitation should be the most important function of prison, next to acting as a deterrent. And it is the 'duty of the state' to rehabilitate those who enter the system.

Sentencing must change. Short sentences are more likely to lead to reoffending, and there needs to be better sentencing. There must be research into the way current sentencing works.

Children who end up in prison have often been in care. They have been looked after but have received little affection. This leads them to finding a sense of belonging in gang culture. Sentencing for children must be about their needs, so they do not reoffend.

A large percentage of people in prison suffer from mental health problems and learning difficulties. Prisons must meet the needs of these people more effectively.

1. Which of the following did the public believe?   *(1 mark)*
   A. ☐ People are let out or prison early because they have behaved well.
   B. ☑ People are let out of prison early because it is too expensive.
   C. ☐ People are afraid of prison.
   D. ☐ People are locked in their cells all day.

2. Which of the following does Michael Gove believe?   *(1 mark)*
   A. ☐ Short sentences are best.
   B. ☐ Few people in prison have learning difficulties.
   C. ☐ More people should be in prison.
   D. ☑ Prisons should rehabilitate people.

3. Analyse the sources to identify two views which the writers disagree about. *(2 marks)*

Sentencing: Lord Ashcroft's report suggests that sentencing should be longer. Michael Gove wants sentencing to be reviewed and research needs to be done.

The purpose of prison: Lord Ashcroft's report says it should be a proper punishment or a deterrent to reoffending. Michael Gove thinks it should be about rehabilitation.

4. Which writer do you agree with more? Explain your answer, referring to the arguments made in both sources. *(12 marks)*

I agree with Michael Gove because he wants to reduce the number of people in prison and find ways of stopping them reoffending.

> The student clearly sets out their point of view.

Sending people to prison makes them more likely to reoffend than sentences that keep them in the community. People lose contact with their families when they are in prison and it makes it harder for them to get a job when they come out.

> The student is using their own knowledge to build their argument.

Lord Ashcroft's report suggests that people should be locked up for longer. This will just make things worse. They will be more likely to return to prison.

> The student is using evidence from the sources to support their argument.

Mr Gove also wants to concentrate on rehabilitation. He thinks this is the duty of the state. It will help people to earn a living when they get out so they are less likely to reoffend. Many people in prison have difficulty reading and writing so education is important. Others have mental health problems so they need looking after rather than just being punished. Lord Ashcroft's report says that life in prison should be more unpleasant so people won't want to go back. If people have all these difficulties they are unlikely to be able to look after themselves after a long prison sentence.

Lord Ashcroft's report says people are let out because it costs too much to keep them in prison. If offenders are rehabilitated and do not return to prison, the costs of running the prisons will fall anyway.

> The student is challenging the logic of the argument.

Extended writing

'Breaking the law is never justified.'

How far do you agree with this view?

Give reasons for your opinion, showing that you have considered other points of view.

In your answer, you could consider:

- reasons for keeping the law
- reasons for breaking the law.

I don't think we should break the law because if we do, life will be difficult for us all. Laws are made to protect people from the actions of others. They mean that the actions of others do not limit our human rights. If everyone broke the law, life would be very difficult. Nothing would be safe and we would be afraid of what might happen next.

> The student sets out the main reason why we should keep the law.

Some people just keep the law because they don't want to be shown up in public. This means that breaking the law and the threat of punishment has a deterrent effect. Court cases are made public so people would be ashamed of their actions.

On the other hand, sometimes laws are broken for good reasons.

> This shows that the student is about to look at the other point of view. It helps the examiner to recognise that you have followed the instruction in the question.

There have been times when the law was unfair to some groups of people in society. Women had to fight for the vote – and broke the law in order to draw attention to their case. People of colour had to fight for equal rights and they broke the law for the same reasons.

People today still protest in ways that break the law. Members of Greenpeace, for example, break the law sometimes when they protest about environmental issues. When they have been taken to court, sometimes they have been let off because the judge thinks their actions were justified.

If someone is in danger, you might need to break the law to help them. You might need to drive too fast if you need to get to a hospital, for example. But you must make sure you do not hurt anyone when you are speeding.

> The student is giving several examples to support their argument.
> Each one has a specific example to make their ideas clear.

To sum up, I think that breaking the law is usually wrong but there are some occasions when it is necessary. You must know that you are doing it and why you are doing it. It must not be just for convenience and you must not hurt anyone else.

> Giving a clear conclusion helps to show that you have answered the question.

Power and influence

Getting you thinking

Engaging young people

In Bromyard, Worcestershire, councillors decided to support young people in the community. They felt it was important for young people to have high self-esteem and a sense of belonging if the community was to build a future for the next generation and continue to thrive. Young people were involved in discussing a new youth club and a drop-in café, and improving transport. They also took the lead in a number of areas and helped to publicise what was going on.

Actions

- Young people are running a monthly teenage disco in the local Falcon Hotel.

- The new Youth of Bromyard forum has held a number of meetings to explore issues that are important to young people and to organise activities.

- Councillors have convened the youth service, schools, the Bromyard Centre, the Hope Family Centre and the Conquest Theatre to meet each quarter, coordinate their approach and look at how best to support young people with projects.

1 What effect are these young people having on their community?

2 How do you think the young people felt about their community?

3 What effect do you think being involved in the community had on the young people?

4 Do you think they are more likely to become involved in the political life of the community – such as joining a youth council or becoming a councillor themselves?

Who participates?

Many people do join in the political life of their communities. Without them, we wouldn't have most of the services that we expect. Some people use their expertise in the roles they hold; others just want to support their community. These are some of the sorts of people who participate in their communities:

- people such as local government officials, police officers, health professionals and teachers who use their expertise

- people holding elected office, such as councillors and MPs

- community workers and activists

- people who are involved in politics

- people who are committed party supporters

- people who are committed to a cause

- people who are concerned about a particular situation

- well-educated, knowledgeable and confident people

- older and retired people with time to spare.

Why do people participate?

Being a member of clubs when you are a child

Your upbringing

Wanting to give back to the community

Life experiences

Political ambitions

Wanting to make a difference

Cultural background

Concern about a specific issue

People who volunteer in the community sometimes decide to become more involved. As their expertise develops, they want to take on tasks that are more of a challenge. This is also true of people who work in social work, healthcare, youth work, community development, housing and education.

People who have suffered some sort of harm, such as domestic abuse, sometimes want to campaign for other people. Faith can also be a motivating factor in participating.

People's involvement can begin with encouragement from family members, friends, colleagues or acquaintances who are already participating.

What are the barriers?

Although many people want to join in, they often find the process frustrating. Many people prefer to be involved in less formal organisations. These tend to be grassroots groups in which decisions are made collectively. People find such organisations motivating as they evolve and people's views count.

By joining formal organisations such as the local council, people can be perceived to be abandoning their communities because they are often working on a bigger picture. This might be the whole town or the county.

There are also practical barriers to people participating in their community. These include lack of time, lack of awareness, the timing of meetings and lack of childcare facilities. People from faith groups may find it difficult if they have religious differences with other people involved.

Young people between the ages of 18 and 26 participate less than others. It is thought that they prefer to deal with single issues, like the environment, rather than formal politics.

Check your understanding

1 Why are people more likely to participate later in life if they have been members of organisations in their youth?
2 Why do people want to participate in the life of their community?
3 What are the barriers?

Action

Find out whether there is a youth council where you live. What does it do?

Another point of view

'People only participate in the life of their community for their own benefit.'

Getting you thinking

Many people follow what is happening in politics

- Less than half have engaged in a political action other than voting or signing a petition.
- But nearly two-thirds (65 per cent) follow political news on a daily basis.
- And half say they sometimes talk about politics with family and friends.

Voter turnout in general elections

2015	66.1%
2010	65.1%
2005	61.4%
2001	59.4%
1997	71.4%
1992	77.7%

Which organisations do people belong to?

	2004 (%)	2014 (%)
Political party		
Belong, actively participate	1	1
Belong, don't participate	9	7
A trade union, business or professional association		
Belong, actively participate	5	5
Belong, don't participate	17	16
A church or other religious organisation		
Belong, actively participate	16	12
Belong, don't participate	18	12
A sports, leisure or cultural group		
Belong, actively participate	23	26
Belong, don't participate	6	6

Source: Natcen Social Research

1 What has been happening to the number of people who vote in general elections?
2 How do we know that many people follow politics?
3 List the organisations people belong to in order of membership.
4 List the organisations people belong to in order of participation.
5 Why do you think there is a difference?

Voting

Being able to vote is very important. If you can't vote, you have no say in what goes on in the country where you live. Voting was originally limited to male landowners. By 1884, most men got the vote. All women did not get the vote until 1928. The government only started to provide free healthcare and education for all after everyone could vote. In 1969 the voting age was lowered to 18 - and many people today would like it to be lowered to 16.

As you saw in 'Getting you thinking', the number of people voting in a general election fell but is rising again. There is much debate about how people can be encouraged to vote. Here are some suggestions.

- They could vote by post.
- They could vote before election day.
- They could vote on Sunday.
- They could vote online.
- They could vote at the supermarket.
- They could be made to vote – legally.

Which of these suggestions do you think might help increase **turnout**?

Joining a political party

If you are interested in politics, you might decide to join the party that holds views closest to your own. You found out about the views of the two main parties on page 61. The major political parties all have youth sections. Organisations encourage young people to take part because they want people to stay committed to their party later on in life. If you want to find out about the parties, have a look at their websites, where you will find their manifestos and information about their youth sections.

If you join, you will be able to take part in campaigning at election time and help to shape policy. You will also be working alongside those who share your beliefs and values, and help your party succeed.

Standing for election

In Theme B you found out why Scott Mann stood for election for North Cornwall. He wanted to make a difference. This is the main reason most people's decide to stand.

Many people first stand for election for their local council. Some then decide to try to become an MP. Others choose to stand for election to the European Parliament.

To stand for the UK Parliament you must be:

- 18 years old or over
- a British citizen
- or a citizen of the Republic of Ireland
- or a citizen of a Commonwealth country who is free to live in the UK.

You cannot stand if you are:

- a member of the police force
- a member of the armed forces
- a civil servant, judge or a peer who can sit in the House of Lords.

Action

Find out from your local councillor, MP or MEP why they decided to stand for election.

Another point of view

'Voting should be compulsory.'

Check your understanding

1 What has happened to turnout in elections?
2 Why should people vote?
3 How could you persuade more people to vote?
4 Why do people join political parties?

Key terms

turnout: the percentage of people who vote in an election

4.3 Putting on the pressure

Getting you thinking

'I will never forget the day when Jay, a boy from the village, was killed. He wasn't the first person to be hit by a car that was speeding through the village. The council seemed to think that 40 mph was quite slow enough, but drivers always thought they could get away with more. What we really needed was a 30 mph limit and some rumble strips so everyone noticed.

When Jay died, I realised it was time to act. I started a petition. There were copies in all the local shops, in the pub, and with all the local organisations. Soon we had over 5000 signatures and we were ready to make our mark.

I took the advice of our local councillor, who suggested that I should go to the council meeting to make my point. I sent a letter and the petition in advance so they would be prepared. At the meeting I stood up and explained what we were asking for. The council members listened carefully.

The council members understood what we wanted and why we wanted it. Within a few months, we, like other villages, had the 30mph limit that would make our lives safer.'

Why was it a good idea to:

1 organise a petition

2 talk to the local councillor

3 send a letter and the petition before the meeting

4 go to the meeting in person?

Making your voice heard

People who want to change things have a variety of options. They might join an **interest group or pressure group**. These groups usually have one objective and want to influence the decisions of people in government, businesses or other organisations.

Taking action

When people are publically supporting an issue, it is known as **advocacy**.

When people are trying to persuade a politician or government, it is known as **lobbying**.

They may use **direct action** to bring about change. The aim is to stop people in their tracks so they have to take notice. Protesters against fracking, for example, superglued themselves to one company's office windows. The company had to take notice! Demonstrations that bring cities to a halt certainly catch the attention of the media and governments.

Indirect action is about persuading politicians or other organisations to change their minds by discussion. It might involve writing letters, producing leaflets or holding meetings. A petition on the government website can have influence. If you get 10 000 signatures, you will get a response from the government. If you get 100 000, your issue may get a debate in Parliament.

You will find out how individuals can hold those in power to account.

4.3 Putting on the pressure

Getting your voice heard

The key to getting your voice heard is to put together a campaign that reaches as many people as possible.

Is there a group of people who care about the issue?

Organise the group and give people responsibilities.

Is the message clear?

Make sure that everyone understands what you are trying to achieve.

Who do you need to talk to?

Find out who is responsible for the things you want to change.

Have you got good evidence?

Do you need a petition to show that lots of people care about the issue? Have you got the facts and figures right?

Is there a local radio station or newspaper?

Local radio stations and papers are always looking for news. How do you get in touch with them?

How do you get the message across?

You might hold a demonstration to get lots of attention. Your leaflets will tell everyone what you want to change. A press release will make sure the media knows what's happening. You will need to fit the method to the audience that you are trying to influence.

Can you make your argument more persuasive?

Look at all the material you have. Test it out on people. Make sure that the key points are very clear. Are there any key issues that will make people take notice? Use them!

Action

Is there a local issue that you really care about? Work out what you would do in order to change things. This will be good preparation for your Citizenship action.

Check your understanding

1 What are advocacy and lobbying

2 What actions can people take if they want to change things? Give some examples of your own.

Another point of view

'People should mind their own business'.

Key terms

advocacy: publicly supporting an issue or proposal

direct action: action to bring about change, such as demonstrations or strikes

indirect action: making your case by persuasion rather than action

interest group or pressure group: a group of people that tries to change public opinion or government policy to its own views or beliefs

lobbying: trying to persuade a politician or the government to change the law or take a particular action

Getting you thinking

What are they doing?

SMASH stands for Swindon Mentoring And Self Help. It aims to support vulnerable young people who need help achieving their full social, emotional, health and educational potential. The overall aim of the project is to increase their potential for achievement in the future.

The charity depends on volunteers who want to give something back to the community. SMASH matches a volunteer to an individual they get on with and who has similar interests. They commit to meeting once a week for a year. It works well because the mentors are not officials or family, so it's often easier to talk.

All sorts of problems

- Trouble with the police?
- Problems at home?
- Problems with friends?
- Problems with confidence or anger management?
- Trouble at school?
- Maybe you just need someone you can talk to.

1 What sort of organisation is SMASH?
2 Why might young people want help?
3 How are the mentors making a difference to their community?
4 Why is it important to help these young people?
5 Why do you think people become mentors?
6 Why do you think communities benefit from the help of volunteers?

Taking action

The people who set up SMASH were working together to offer a service to their local community. The mentors are taking individual action to help people in their local community. Each young person who is helped by SMASH knows that their mentor is giving up their own time and isn't being paid – so they must really care.

You will discover how individuals and groups can make a difference in their community.

4.4 Making a difference

Why volunteer?

People volunteer for all sorts of reasons, as the chart below suggests. Most people get personal satisfaction from seeing the results of their contribution to the community. They really enjoy the activity too. Many feel that it helps them because they develop their skills.

I wanted to improve things, help people	53
The cause was important to me	41
I had time to spare	41
I wanted to meet people	30
It connected with needs/interests of family or friends	29
There was a need in the community	29
Friends/family did it	21
To learn new skills	19
Part of my religious belief	17
To help get on in my career	7
Had received voluntary help myself	4
Already involved in the organisation	2
Connected with my interests, hobbies	2
To give something back	1

An organisation called Volunteering Matters helps people to volunteer. It runs programmes, led by volunteers, to help communities across the country.

Action

Find out about volunteering activities that are going on in your local area. Work out who benefits from the activities. Make a presentation to the class or a larger group about how the community works together.

Another point of view

'I don't want to give up my time to help others.'

Born to Be – Deutsche Bank's youth engagement strategy

Rahat Hadi works for Deutsche Bank and volunteers to support a young student at a school in East London.

'For the past year I've been working with an 11-year-old boy from Syria. To begin with, I had to earn his trust and build a friendship with him. He had faced many challenges before arriving in London and it took some time for him to connect with a complete stranger. He now loves reading his favourite books, has extended his vocabulary and passes reading tests with ease.

I've had the opportunity to make a difference to someone's life, and contribute to my local community. It's also enabled me to develop my patience and negotiation skills. As a result, I now deal more effectively with conflict resolution in my role at Deutsche Bank.'

Born to Be targets 11–18 year olds, focusing on breaking the cycle of youth unemployment through early intervention.

The value to the economy

If all the work done by **volunteers** had to be paid for, it would cost more than £50 billion. This clearly helps communities to help people who need support. Without the volunteers, they might miss out because there might not be enough money to pay for the support.

Money is not the only benefit to the economy. It brings people closer together and helps communities to become more sustainable.

Check your understanding

1 What is volunteering?
2 Who benefits from volunteering?
3 Why do people volunteer?
4 Why do some businesses encourage their staff to volunteer?
5 What impact does volunteering have on communities?

Key terms   **volunteer:** someone who works for free for a community

4.5 Getting out the vote

Getting you thinking

My vote won't make a difference.

I'm not interested in politics.

I don't know enough about it all.

The parties and candidates are all the same.

I can't get to the polling station.

1 Why do you think people feel this way?

2 Suggest ways in which each of these issues can be overcome.

3 How can we help young people to be more interested in voting?

Registering to vote

If you want to vote, you have to register first. You need to prove who you are and register either through the Post Office or online. Individual registration was introduced to prevent fraud, as some people had been filling in postal votes for people registered at their house. It takes a bit more effort than when one person could register everyone in the household. It means that students, for example, have to register themselves independently of their family.

There are now campaigns to encourage people to register. Universities and schools all play a role in this.

It has been suggested that registration should be automatic, perhaps based on your National Insurance number, but some people fear that this would lead to fraud.

Making politics more engaging

Many organisations, from Parliament itself to pressure groups that want to support democracy, have done research into ways of increasing interest in politics. They have come to the following three conclusions:

1 More information

When asked, many people said they did not have enough information to vote. When people who hadn't voted were asked what would help:

- 16 per cent said receiving a leaflet
- 12 per cent said a personal visit from a candidate
- 12 per cent said more information about how and where to vote
- 11 per cent said more information on how to get a postal vote
- 6 per cent said receiving an email from a candidate.

There is a lot of information to help people decide which party to vote for, but it is often not easy to find. On page 61, you found out about a website that would help you.

2 Being recognised

It also seems important to be recognised for voting. This might mean a sticker to tell everyone, 'I have voted' or a pin on Facebook.

3 Education

Citizenship education seems to be an important factor in voting. The more people learn about the system and why everyone should be involved, the more likely they are to vote later on. This links with lowering the voting age to16. Having learned all about how the country works, students are ready and prepared to vote.

Proportional representation (PR)

Many people think there is no point in voting if they live in a constituency where the party they support is never elected. PR means that every vote counts. Look back at page 58 to find out more about it.

The Youth Parliament at work

How can I vote?

In Theme B, Democracy at work in the UK, you learned about some of the issues related to voting. Many of the people questioned about how they might be encouraged to vote suggested that they wanted to know more about the process and how to go about it.

Here is a range of possible ways to help.

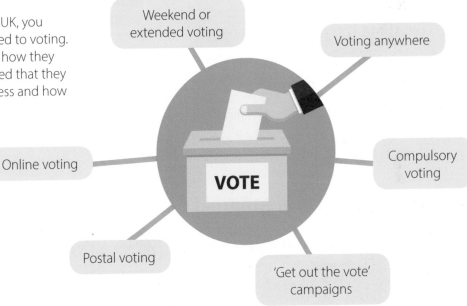

- Weekend or extended voting
- Voting anywhere
- Online voting
- Compulsory voting
- Postal voting
- 'Get out the vote' campaigns

VOTE

You will learn more about digital democracy on the next page.

Check your understanding

1 Why do some people not bother to vote?

2 Why do you think people should vote?

3 How can people be encouraged to register to vote?

4 What changes do non-voters want in order for them to vote?

5 What might be done to encourage them to vote?

6 Why might proportional representation help?

7 Why would citizenship education help?

Action

Debate the motion that 'My vote makes no difference, so it's not worth bothering.'

Another point of view

'If people don't vote, they can't complain about what's happening.'

Getting you thinking

A modern way of voting

Estonia, an EU member on the Baltic Sea, has been using internet voting for more than 10 years. In 2015, more than 30 per cent of voters cast their votes through e-voting.

This is how it works. During the pre-voting period, voters log on to the system using a ID card or Mobile ID, and cast a ballot. The voter's identity is removed from the ballot before it reaches the National Electoral Commission for counting, thereby ensuring anonymity.

The system is much cheaper than a paper-based election.

But what are the problems?

The Estonian system needs electronic ID cards – which have been rejected in the UK. There are also serious questions about its security.

Will the system crash? Estonia is a small country. If everyone decided to vote at the same moment, there could be problems.

Could the system be hacked by malicious groups or foreign governments that want to disrupt the election?

1 What do you think the advantages of e-voting might be?

2 What are the disadvantages?

3 Do you think voters in the UK would be happy to use a system like this?

The pros and cons of political parties using social media

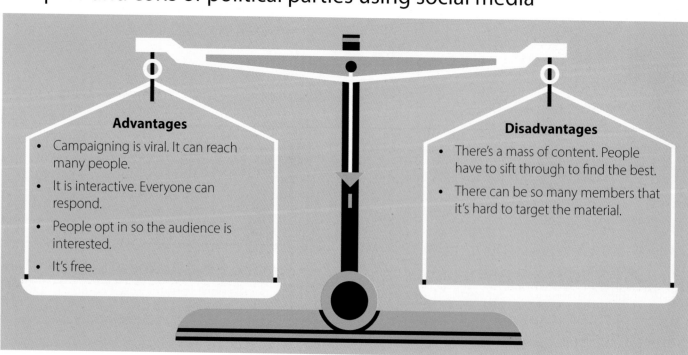

Advantages

- Campaigning is viral. It can reach many people.
- It is interactive. Everyone can respond.
- People opt in so the audience is interested.
- It's free.

Disadvantages

- There's a mass of content. People have to sift through to find the best.
- There can be so many members that it's hard to target the material.

Email and texts

Many parties use emails and texts to connect with potential voters. They must get your permission and conform to certain rules. It's wise not to swamp people with messages because they quickly get bored.

Online campaigning

Before an election in the USA, television is full of adverts for political parties. They often criticise the other candidates rather than giving a positive image of the one responsible for the advert. In the UK, political parties are not allowed to advertise on television, but they are on the internet. Before an election, the parties pour out adverts and videos to support their cause. It's much cheaper than television advertising and can reach lots of potential voters.

The parties can measure how many people are interested in their campaign from looking at the number of Twitter followers and Facebook likes. They can also pick up issues that engage voters or worry them, so it's useful to help them direct their campaigns.

Young people seemed to have lost interest in politics, but digital campaigning may have recaptured their interest. As you have already seen, turnout in general elections has been rising, so digital campaigning may have helped.

Candidates must be careful when using Twitter or Facebook because a hasty comment can lead to their downfall. One MP Tweeted a picture taken while he was preparing a speech before the general election. He wanted to present himself as an ordinary chap – eating a burger and chips. Unfortunately, his meal came from a posh burger restaurant rather than the usual high street shops. It didn't give the message he had intended.

Making the most of petitions

You have discovered how people can use online petitions to get their message out for politicians to see. They are useful for the political parties too. By looking at the e-petitions on the government website, a party can see which issues are worrying people and how much support they have.

Action

Go to YouTube and do some research to find out how the political parties have used it to get their message across.

Check your understanding

1 What are the advantages and disadvantages of online voting?

2 What are the advantages and disadvantages to political parties of using social media?

3 Why must political parties be careful when using emails and texts?

4 Why do political parties use online campaigning?

5 Look at the photograph and explain why the apps can be useful to a political party.

6 Why do MPs need to be careful when they Tweet?

7 Which age group may have been encouraged to take an interest and vote by parties campaigning online?

Another point of view

'Digital campaigning just trivialises politics.'

Key terms   **digital democracy:** the use of online methods to support election campaigns and voting

Journalists protest about limits on the press.

Azerbaijan v Norway

Azerbaijan is a country on the Caspian Sea. It has even hosted the Eurovision Song Contest. But all is not well. Since 1993, the same family has run the country with an iron fist.

From a very early age, children in Azerbaijan learn about how the Heydar Aliyev, the father of the president, brought stability to the country. This made him very popular. Children in school even recite poems about him.

Ilham Aliyev took over as president when his father died. He was already Prime Minister and vice chairman of the national oil company.

Although there was an election, observers were very critical of the campaign. There was voter intimidation, violence and media bias. International media was not allowed into the country. Demonstrations by the opposition were met with police violence. There were many arrests.

Ilham runs a country that has great oil wealth. But there is also widespread poverty, much corruption and mass unemployment.

1 What do you think it means to run a country with an 'iron fist'?

2 Why had Heydar Aliyev become very popular?

3 How democratic is Azerbaijan? Explain your answer.

4 How does it compare with democracy in the UK?

5 What difficulties do people face when countries do not have democratic processes?

Degrees of democracy

A country may have elections, but if they are not free and fair, the country is not democratic. In many countries round the world, elections are held but the citizens are not free to vote as they might wish. The table shows how different regions of the world compare. How democratic they are is marked out of 10.

Region	2014
Asia and Australasia	5.70
Eastern Europe	5.58
Latin America	6.36
Middle East and North Africa	3.65
North America	8.59
Western Europe	8.41
Sub-Saharan Africa	4.34
World average	*5.55*

In comparison with a democratic government, a **dictator**:

- rules by making law himself

- is an absolute ruler of a state

- ignores the rule of law

- often gains power through fraud or overthrowing the government

- may develop a cult of personality

- may be autocratic, oppressive, despotic or tyrannical.

You will compare the power of citizens to participate in different countries.

4.7 Does your vote count?

Norway is top of the list of the most democratic countries. They are judged on eight points.

1 Almost all adult citizens have the right to vote.

2 Almost all adult citizens are eligible for public office.

3 Political leaders have the right to compete for votes.

4 Elections are free and fair.

5 All citizens are free to form and join political parties and other organisations.

6 All citizens are free to express themselves on all political issues.

7 The media is free to express views about politics and they are protected by law.

8 Government policies depend on votes.

Norwegians celebrate their Constitution Day.

1 What role do you think the Norwegians have in running their country?

2 How is this different from Azerbaijan?

3 Which country would you prefer to live in? Why?

4 What does your answer to the last question tell you about the importance of using your vote?

Check your understanding

1 How is the life of people in Azerbaijan limited?

2 How would you describe the democratic role of people in

a Azerbaijan

b Norway?

3 Why is freedom of the press so important?

4 What does 'ignores the rule of law' mean?

5 Why are people likely to be better off in a country that is more democratic?

Action

Make a list of countries on different continents and find out how democratic they are.

Another point of view

'People in power know better than the rest of us, so they should be allowed to get on and rule the country.'

Key terms

dictator: a national leader who makes all the decisions for the country, without reference to the population

Getting you thinking

Scope: Our purpose . . . .

'Scope exists to make this country a place where disabled people have the same opportunities as everyone else. Until then, we'll be here. We provide support, information and advice to more than a quarter of a million disabled people and their families every year. We raise awareness of the issues that matter. And with your support, we'll keep driving change across society until this country is great for everyone.'

Stop HS2: About us . . . .

'Stop HS2 is the national grassroots campaign against the proposed new High Speed Two railway. We formed after several months of studying the HS2 proposals in depth.

Our mission is:

- to stop High Speed Two by persuading the government to scrap the HS2 proposal

- to facilitate local and national campaigning against High Speed Two.

Our supporters come from a wide range of backgrounds and from across the political spectrum. Over 108 000 people signed our original petition, which we took to Downing Street in October 2011, on the day of a House of Commons debate on HS2.

Stop HS2 supporters work with a variety of international, national and local groups and individuals, with the intention of getting HS2 cancelled.

Our aim is to be inclusive and empowering. We actively encourage individuals and groups to campaign against HS2 in a variety of ways.'

STOP HS2

1 How are Scope and Stop HS2 similar?

2 How are they different?

3 Why are they likely to be more effective than individuals working alone?

4 How might they be carrying out their campaigning?

What is a voluntary organisation?

Voluntary organisations are usually run by people with a mission to change something. Scope, in 'Getting you thinking', wants to make life better for disabled people. Stop HS2 is different because it wants to prevent a government proposal from happening.

There is a close link between voluntary organisations and pressure groups – they both want to change aspects of life.

Because voluntary organisations and pressure groups have a mission, they work hard to persuade the government to make changes to accept their proposals. They also want to influence public opinion in order to encourage the government to listen.

In 'Making a difference' on pages 114 and 115, you found out about how people worked together to improve their communities. One group was helping disadvantaged children. Another group was supporting a school. Here we have examples of people wanting to change government policy and challenge injustice.

You will explore how groups and organisations provide support for groups in society.

4.8 Supporting society

What is a charity?

A **charity** is an organisation set up to provide help and raise money for those in need. 'Need' can mean support in all sorts of ways. Charities range from organisations that offer advice for teachers to ones that provide clean water to villages in Africa.

Public support

The government also offers support for the public. It provides **public institutions**, such as schools, colleges, courts, libraries, hospitals and other places that are run for the public to use. It also provides a range of **public services** that help people in their everyday lives. Elections give us the opportunity to have our say on what we want. Some parties want to spend more than others on the provision of services.

Here are some of those services.

Education · Libraries · Policing · Emergency services · Public housing · Healthcare · Social services · Court services · Town planning · Radio and television · Refuse collection

---

Action

Explore a voluntary organisation in your area. How does it help the community? How could you help the organisation?

Another point of view

'The government should look after all groups in society.'

Check your understanding

1 What is a voluntary organisation?
2 What do voluntary organisations do?
3 What is a charity?
4 How does the government help?

Key terms

charity: an organisation set up to provide help and raise money for those in need
public institutions: organisations provided by the government, like schools and hospitals
public services: services provided by the state, like policing, education and refuse collection
voluntary organisations: bodies whose activities are carried out for reasons other than profit, but which do not include any public or local authority funding

4.9 Trade unions and the protection of people at work

Getting you thinking

The Tolpuddle Martyrs

In the 1830s, farm workers' lives were hard and getting worse. They were threatened by more cuts to their pay. Some fought back. They broke the new threshing machines that would have taken their jobs, but this brought harsh punishments.

In 1834, a group of farm workers in Tolpuddle, Dorset, formed a trade union in order to fight for their jobs and pay. Although unions were legal and growing fast, the six leaders were arrested and sentenced to seven years' transportation to Australia – a very harsh punishment. A massive protest swept across the country and many people organised petitions and protest meetings to demand their freedom.

The campaign won and the Tolpuddle Martyrs, as they had become known, returned home in triumph.

Today, people still celebrate the Tolpuddle Martyrs with a festival each year. The freedom to join a trade union has become a basic human right.

1 Why did the Tolpuddle farm workers join together to fight their cause?

2 Why have trade unions grown since the days of the Tolpuddle Martyrs?

3 Why do you think people join trade unions today?

The origin of trade unions

People fought long and hard for the right to join together to fight for rights in the workplace. Going on strike was punished by a sentence to hard labour.

Throughout the 1800s, workers fought for their rights until they could be ignored no longer. Trade organisations were formed by engineers, miners and agricultural labourers. Some were national or regional organisations.

In 1868, the Trades Union Congress – or TUC, as it is more commonly known – was founded in Manchester. By 1880, there were more than a million trade union members. People at last had the right to fight for their rights by collective action.

People's rights today

In 'Fair play at work' on page 37, you were introduced to the ways people's rights are protected at work. Trade unions have paid a large part in the development of these laws. Today, employers and trade unions usually try to come to an agreement when negotiating pay and conditions. Sometimes they do not succeed and the trade union calls a strike. All the members are entitled to vote on the decision. If there is a majority, the strike will go ahead. **Collective bargaining**, like this, makes the position of employees much stronger. Some people belong to **staff associations**, which can have the same role in protecting them. All people at work should have a contract, but conflicts can still arise.

What if it goes wrong?

People can be **dismissed** if they are unable to do their job properly or have been involved in any misconduct, such as fighting, discrimination, deliberate damage or theft.

People can be made **redundant** when their job has ended and no one is being taken on to replace them. If this happens, the person will be paid at least the equivalent of one month's pay for every year they have held the job if they are between 22 and 41.

Resolving conflict

If there is a disagreement between the employer and the employee, there are steps that can be taken to solve the problem.

If the employee is a member of a trade union, it will advise them and argue their case with their employer.

If it can't be sorted out, the case can be taken to an **employment tribunal**. This is a type of court of law. It has the power to fine the business and make it pay damages to the employee if it finds that the employee was not to blame. If the dismissed person belongs to a union, they can seek advice from it and the union can represent them at the tribunal.

Before going to a tribunal, the parties must contact **ACAS**, an organisation that will try to help resolve the dispute.

An employment tribunal: a more informal court of law

Check your understanding

1 Why did workers want to join together in trade unions?
2 Why do you think employers didn't want this to happen?
3 What reason can be given for dismissal?
4 What is the difference between dismissal and redundancy?
5 What can an employee do if they feel they have been treated unfairly?

Action

Look in a local or national paper to see if there are any reports of an industrial tribunal. What was the issue? Who won? Why? Had one side acted irresponsibly? If so, explain how.

Another point of view

'The employer is always right.'

Key terms

ACAS: an organisation that tries to resolve disputes between employers and employees

collective bargaining: negotiating the terms of employment between an employer and a group of workers

dismissal: when an employer ends an employee's contract of employment

employment tribunal: a type of court dealing only with disagreements over employment laws

redundancy: when a person loses their job because the job doesn't need to be done any more

staff associations: associations of employees with some of the functions of a trade union, such as representing their members in discussions with management

Getting you thinking

- Let's all chill out together this evening.
- Let's plan a holiday.
- Let's find out if my team won.
- Let's find out the latest news.
- Let's choose which new car we want.
- Let's have a quiet night at home.
- Let's find out about Fair Trade.

1 Most of the activities above can be done on the internet. Choose one other way you might carry each one out and explain your choices.

2 Do you believe or trust what you learn from one kind of media more than from another?

3 How do you decide what to trust?

4 What effect does reading, seeing or hearing material that you don't trust have on your views?

Mass media

The **media** has become a massive industry over the last 50 years. One hundred years ago, newspapers were the only form of information about what was happening in people's locality, the UK and beyond. In the days when many people couldn't read, they only knew what they were told by other people.

Today, there is information everywhere. Newspapers and magazines are widely available. You could watch television 24 hours a day. Cable television and the digital revolution have changed things even more. They provide news, entertainment and education whenever you want it, even from your mobile phone.

Viewers, listeners and readers

Habits change. A hundred years ago, politicians could expect to speak to a packed hall at election time. There was no television, so it was the only way people could ever see who they were voting for. Today, the numbers watching party political broadcasts are in decline. Perhaps there is so much exposure that people are no longer curious about who governs them.

As new methods of communication arrive, people move on. When radio was introduced, families would sit together listening carefully. When television broadcasts started, radio listening declined. Now we have over 50 television channels, so each company has to work extra hard to attract our attention. With most families having the internet at home or on the road, television watching may take different forms. What will come next?

Who does what?

Despite all the changes, people still buy newspapers, books and magazines, listen to the radio and watch television. The choice of media means that we select the ways of finding out information that suit us best. Although the patterns change, most people use most media most of the time. They simply adjust the amount of time they spend on each one.

Adult participation in selected leisure activities (%): by age							
Age	16–19	20–24	25–29	30–44	45–59	60–69	70 +
Watching TV	100	99	99	99	99	99	99
Listening to radio	92	93	93	92	89	82	76
Listening to music	98	97	95	91	83	71	57
Reading books	63	67	66	65	67	64	64

Source: Social Trends

The internet

Political parties use the internet to provide information and organise online surveys of **public opinion**. People might want to vote if they can join in debates and have easier access to information.

Products for people

All forms of media aim to provide what the customer wants. There are television channels aimed at young people and others aimed at an older population. There is also a growing number of channels aimed at people with specific interests, ranging from music to gardening, from cooking to history.

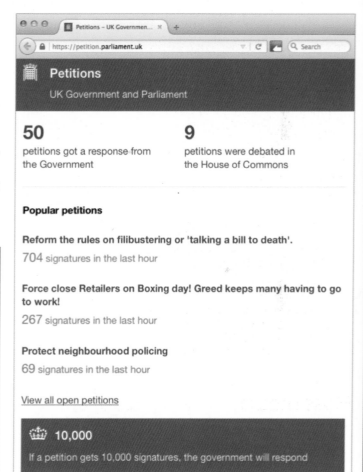

Action

1 Look at a range of papers from the same day. Do they tell the stories in different ways? How are they different?

2 Watch the news on various television channels on the same day. Does each channel give the same picture? Do different channels take a different approach?

3 Do you prefer one newspaper's or television channel's way of telling the story? Do you believe one more than the other? Explain why.

Check your understanding

1 What is meant by 'the media'?
2 How has the media changed over the last 100 years?
3 What does the media provide?
4 Why is the media powerful?

Another point of view

'Newspapers are more powerful now than they were 100 years ago.'

Key terms

media: ways of communicating with large numbers of people
public opinion: views held by the general public on a particular issue

Getting you thinking

Zimbabwe's media control

The Zimbabwean police have banned alternative sources of media and seized short-wave radios. Many Zimbabweans, especially in rural areas, rely on short-wave radio as their main source of information. They also pick up independent and international stations rather than state-run stations.

The police raided the offices of the election watchdog, claiming they were looking for subversive materials, gadgets and illegal immigrants. The offices of a radio station were also raided and 180 solar and kinetic energy-powered radios were seized.

Telegraph journalist arrested

Peta Thornycroft, a journalist on the *Daily Telegraph*, was arrested and accused of publishing false information. If convicted, she could face two years in prison. Journalists continue to be harassed through attacks from senior politicians, unlawful arrests and threats of closure.

Journalists protest in Namibia about the clampdown on press freedom in Zimbabwe, the country next door. They would have been arrested if they had protested in Zimbabwe.

Despite Zimbabwe's new constitution, there are still laws that control the media.

1 How is the media being controlled in Zimbabwe?
2 Why do you think the government brought these laws into force?
3 What effect do you think this has on life in Zimbabwe and the outcome of elections?
4 How do you think these laws affect the way other countries view Zimbabwe?
5 Why is it important for the media to be free to report on events?
6 Do you think there should be any limit on what the media can say?

What is freedom?

'Everyone has the right to the freedom of opinion and expression; this right includes freedom to hold opinions without interference and to seek, receive and impart information and ideas through any media, regardless of frontiers.'

Universal Declaration of Human Rights

One of every human being's rights is to have their say. If they don't like the government, they should be free to say so. If people think the government should spend more or less on health, education or defence, laws should not prevent them from saying so. If people want to know what is going on, they should be free to find out. Information and data should not be kept secret unless there is a good reason. In a democracy, people need to be able to hear others' points of view and know what is going on if they are to use their vote effectively.

Why control the press?

If information is kept from people, they will find it hard to decide whether the government is keeping its promises or breaking the law in order to stay in power. If a government is determined to stay in power, preventing people from knowing the truth can be very effective. **Censorship** means that people will only know what the government wants them to know.

Press freedom is often the first thing to go when the government of a country wants to prevent democracy working. A country that controls the press cannot really be democratic. There are examples throughout history. In the last century, the Soviet Union controlled all forms of media. Even today, there are no television channels that are free from government control in Russia. China also has strong controls on what the people are told. There are examples of press control throughout the world.

A voter in Zimbabwe reads a government-owned paper, which accuses the opposition party of terrorism. Media output is controlled by the government.

In Russia the government controls all television output.

Is it ever right to control the media?

When the UK was fighting Argentina over the Falkland Islands in 1981, there was a complete news blackout. Every night a government spokesman appeared on the television and gave a report. He read a message in a slow, serious manner, telling us what the government thought we should know.

When people are caught spying, very often much of the information that is provided in court is not published.

These are both examples of occasions when national security is thought more important than press freedom. Sometimes, by telling people everything, you may be giving the game away. There is, however, always a debate about how much information should be given out.

Check your understanding

1 What does the Universal Declaration of Human Rights have to say about press freedom?

2 Why might a government that wants to be re-elected decide to control the press?

3 Why can democracy not work effectively if the press is controlled?

4 Are there reasons why press freedom should sometimes be limited? Explain your answer.

5 Draw up a list of issues that you think the press should be free to discuss and any that you think it should not be allowed to print stories about. Use your list to draw up a law on press freedom.

Another point of view

'The media must always be free to express a point of view.'

Key terms

censorship: limiting the information given to the general public by the government

press freedom: the ability of the press to give information and express opinion

Getting you thinking

What the papers said…

The Labour Party needed a new leader, so it set about an election in which its members could decide who they wanted. One of the candidates became more popular than expected.

Here are some of the headlines you might have seen.

> **Corbyn too old for election race**

> *Corbyn 'isn't Labour, and can't lead'*

> **What Jeremy Corbyn offers his supporters is clear thinking**

> **Corbyn told to give up race – because he was too close to winning**

> **Oh no!**

> **We'd vote for Corbyn because we've had enough of the others**

> **Corbyn's the only candidate for Labour leader who really believes in something**

1 Which headlines are in favour of Mr Corbyn?

2 Which are against him?

3 Do you think they are trying to influence people? If so why?

4 Do you think the statements are fact or opinion?

Fact and opinion

The headlines in 'Getting you thinking' show how the media can take different views on an issue. Much of the media informs the public about what's going on, but it often puts a spin on the information it offers. When they do this, the report is **biased**.

If, as a reader or viewer, you are aware of the bias of a television programme or newspaper, you can take the bias into account. If not, you may just believe it all.

The BBC has a commitment to being 'independent, accurate and impartial'. People often argue about this, but it is part of the BBC's role in providing a public service.

What leads to bias?

Ownership

A newspaper or television news programme can choose the stories it wants to tell and decide how to tell them. The owners of a paper appoint an editor to run it for them. The **editor** has the

power to make these decisions. Often, an editor is chosen because they have the same points of view as the owner. This means that the way the news is presented reflects the owner point of view. Television news has editors too. They put the programme together in just the same way.

Most newspapers belong to companies owned by shareholders. The objective is to make a profit, so sales are a top priority. Businesses that want to sell their products will buy advertising space in papers with many readers. Lots of sales means lots of advertising, and selling advertising helps to increase profits.

You will find out about how the media informs and influences the public.

4.12 The media: informing or influencing?

Political spin

Politicians often want to be at the top of the news and shown in a good light. Political parties employ **spin-doctors** who write the stories and work hard to get them in the news. You often hear about government spending on health, education or other areas people care about. When **journalists** look carefully, however, they often find that the spending has been announced several times before! This is the work of spin-doctors.

Under control

Every time one media company wants to take over another, the plans are reviewed. If the takeover puts too much power in too few hands, it won't be allowed to go ahead.

The Murdoch family runs companies that control all these media organisations plus lots more around the world.

The Times

The Sunday Times

The Sun

HarperCollins

Sky TV

Twentieth Century Fox

Fox TV

National Geographic Channel

Advertising

Advertising pays for commercial television and the newspapers. If you were the editor, what would you do if you were faced with a story that showed one of your main advertisers in a bad light?

Would you:

- run the story?
- hold it for a day when there were no adverts from that business?
- rewrite the story so it was less critical?
- just ignore it?

It's a tough decision to make.

Action

Compare articles about the same story or event in two different newspapers. Is there a difference in the way the stories are told? Is there any bias?

Another point of view

'The media are always biased.'

Check your understanding

1 What does an editor do?
2 Why are media owners powerful?
3 What factors influence the contents of a newspaper?
4 How is media ownership controlled?

Key terms

biased: in favour one thing over another, unfairly
editor: the person who is responsible for the content of a newspaper, television or radio programme
journalist: a person who gathers news and produces reports for the media
spin-doctor: someone who tries to get certain stories into the public eye and to make bad news sound better

Getting you thinking

1 Identify the different sorts of people in these pictures.

2 What sort of things does the press do to give people cause for complaint?

3 Do you think that these complaints are always justified?

4 Make a list of things you feel the press should not do.

5 Make suggestions about how to stop the press doing this sort of thing.

What are the rules?

Anyone in the public eye can be pestered by the press. People find themselves being looked at through the long lens of a camera and on the front page the next day. Ordinary people who have had some good luck or experienced misfortune are just as vulnerable as the famous.

The media has the right to investigate issues that are in the public interest. Its reports must be accurate and it must not invade people's privacy. The Independent Press Standards Organisation attempts to prevent this invasion of privacy, but it is not always successful. It has drawn up the **Editors' Code of Practice** as guidance for journalists working in the media.

Although it can look at complaints and decide if the code has been broken, it can do little to prevent its happening again.

The wrong side of the law?

Sometimes it's a question of invading people's privacy, but on other occasions it's about the media getting its facts wrong. When this happens, a paper or television channel can find itself in court facing a **libel** or **slander** case.

Laws prevent anyone from making untrue public statements about people. Footballers have challenged people who said they fixed a game and politicians have challenged newspapers that said they received money for asking particular questions in Parliament. *Private Eye*, the magazine that takes a satirical look at the world, often finds itself in court because it has pushed the limits too far.

The Editors' Code of Practice

Newspapers:

- **must not** publish inaccurate, misleading or distorted information or pictures
- **must** give a right to reply to any inaccurate reporting
- **must** respect people's private and family life
- **must not** harass people for information
- **must not** intrude on grief or shock
- **must not** intrude on children during their schooling
- **must not** use hidden bugs to find things out
- **must** avoid prejudice
- **must not** make payments to people involved in criminal cases
- **must not** profit from financial information
- **must not** identify victims of sexual assault
- **must** protect confidential sources.

Popular or quality?

People buy four times more popular papers than quality papers. The quality press tends to take a more serious view of the world and its headlines reflect this. In contrast, on days when dramatic world events are taking place, popular papers have been famous for headlining footballers, sex and money.

Average sales of daily newspapers in the UK

Title	2015	2012
Daily Mirror	863,564	1,077,683
Daily Record	190,668	273,688
Daily Star	424,363	596,108
The Sun	1,836,472	2,519,911
Daily Express	428,075	561,273
Daily Mail	1,623,579	1,920,801
The Daily Telegraph	483,232	570,817
Financial Times	209,800	298,070
The Guardian	171,418	210,660
i	275,674	279,309
The Independent	58,082	90,258
The Times	395,559	400,238
Daily Star - Sunday	265,743	460,720
The Sun on Sunday	1,500,448	2,167,218
Sunday Mail	209,628	319,393
Sunday Mirror	815,431	1,173,269
Sunday People	312,337	499,048
Sunday Express	375,678	513,305
Sunday Post	183,206	272,245
The Mail on Sunday	1,434,875	1,798,205
Independent on Sunday	97,593	121,794
The Observer	192,292	245,430
The Sunday Telegraph	369,917	449,882
The Sunday Times	778,654	918,563

Source: ABC

1 Which is the largest selling quality paper?

2 Which is the largest selling popular paper?

3 Why do you think newspaper owners might be worried?

4 What do you think has happened to the way people find out about the news?

Legal limits

Just like anyone else, the media has to obey laws about decency. Discrimination is against the law and some parts of the media have to be very careful not to overstep the limits. The popular papers find themselves in front of the Independent Press Standards Organisation or in court more often than the quality press. But who is responsible? After all, the more sensational the story, the more we want to buy the paper.

Action

1 What decisions has the Independent Press Standards Organisation made recently? Do you agree with their findings? Why?

2 The i is the only paper which is growing in circulation. Have a look at one and work out why.

Check your understanding

1 How should people's privacy be protected?

2 How effective do you think the Independent Press Standards Organisation is?

3 Can you think of any examples when their rules have been broken?

4 Why is it important for journalists to protect confidential sources of information?

5 How does the law limit what newspapers can print?

Key terms

Editors' Code of Practice: guidelines for the media and journalists about the information they gather and how they obtain and use it

libel: writing incorrect things about people

slander: saying incorrect things about people

Getting you thinking

Cities fit for cycling

After several people had been killed while cycling in London, *The Times* took up the cause. It was prompted by an accident in which one of their journalists was severely injured. 'Cities fit for cycling' is a campaign that has changed people's views on cyclists and made the roads safer.

Safer lorries

A British company has invented a new digital roadmap that directs HGVs to their destinations, avoiding places where cyclists come under threat on the route.

Left turns, where cyclists are in the lorries' blind spot, are the biggest threat. The software, which runs to satnavs and smartphones, gives lorries a route through a town that only uses right turns.

Safer routes to school

The Welsh government is spending £5 million on safe cycle routes for pupils cycling to school. The fund will be spent on 30 new projects. These will include cycle paths, secure cycle facilities, lighting, crossings and traffic-calming measures.

One school reported that the paths had improved punctuality. One pupil from just over two miles away says it takes him five minutes on his bike, but half an hour on the bus.

1. Why do you think newspapers set up campaigns?

2. Why do you think they can influence people?

3. Why do you think businesses and governments are influenced by such campaigns?

The Pasty Tax

In a recent budget, the Chancellor announced that he was going to put VAT on warm pasties. This caused outrage among pasty lovers. Shops selling pasties were outraged too. If pasties were sold hot, they were taxable, if they were cold, they weren't. Who was to measure how hot they were? The newspapers took up the cause. The government started to look ridiculous – and the proposal was withdrawn.

1 Why do you think the government wanted to tax pasties?

2 Why do you think the public was so outraged?

3 How could the media influence public opinion?

4 Why do you think the government changed its mind?

Great British backdown

Investigation

The media has always taken on issues in society and exposed them to public inspection. The aim is to right wrongs. **Investigative journalism** helps to sell papers as the results of the research are published.

• A recent investigation into the living and working conditions of workers on tea plantations in Assam, India, showed many failures. People were living in poor housing with dreadful sanitation. Their wages were so low that they could not buy enough food for their families. As a result of this investigation, big brand tea companies in the UK have promised to work with the people who run the plantations to improve conditions.

• MPs' large expenses claims were exposed by newspapers. MPs are allowed to claim expenses because they have to live away from home for much of the week. However, some made outrageous claims for second homes. Many were exposed and some ended up in prison. New rules were put in place so MPs cannot do this any more.

When businesses and government come under **scrutiny**, they often change. If businesses are shown in a bad light, they may lose customers. This will hit their profits so they will probably change the way they work.

When the way government works is challenged, it may change its policies or organisation. It fears losing votes at the next election and therefore losing power.

Action

What media investigations are taking place at the moment? Look at the media to see what is concerning journalists. Are they having any effect?

Check your understanding

1 What is the objective of investigative journalism?

2 Why are businesses likely to change the way they work when issues are exposed?

3 Why are governments likely to change their policies when they are exposed?

Another point of view

'Scrutiny by the media is not necessary.'

Key terms

investigative journalism: the deep investigation of a topic of interest, such as serious crimes, political corruption or corporate wrongdoing

scrutiny: to examine something carefully

2 MILLION more jobs | **3 MILLION** new apprenticeships

"A government for **#workingpeople**"

HM Government

the **youth summit**
Our goals. Our voice. Our future.

How **YOU** can get involved on Sat 12th

1 Post a picture/video telling the world how you will help achieve the Global Goals

#YouthSummit
I commit...

2 Follow the story on Snapchat
UKaid
username: DFID_UK

3 Join us LIVE on Twitter &
Periscope
username: DFID_UK

4 View the LIVE STREAM at
theyoutsummit.org
We go LIVE at noon

#Youth Summit

ICS UKaid THE GLOBAL GOALS

Need help to start your own business?

"You can't give up, so many young people are disheartened - they don't realise there's help available if you want to run your own business, like the New Enterprise Allowance."

Jada
Jada Lynton Collection

Department for Work & Pensions

#BusinessisGREAT

The official Facebook page for the UK government highlights government information and support.

1 What sort of information is the government providing on its Facebook page?

2 Why do you think it has a Facebook page?

3 Why do you think it uses Facebook rather than other media?

4 Can you think of reasons why Facebook is useful to the government?

What is public opinion?

Public opinion sums up the views of the population. It can give the government strong messages about people's views on current issues. This can affect how laws are changed. Governments aim to be re-elected and therefore generally take public opinion into account when they make decisions.

Opinion polls are commissioned to find out what people think. They may be organised by people who want their views heard and think some hard evidence of people's views will help to persuade the government to listen.

Newspapers are always running opinion polls to find out which political party has most public support.

How is public opinion formed?

The public comes under pressure from a wide range of organisations that want to influence how they think. The government, as with its Facebook page, tries hard to persuade us that it is doing the best for us because it would like us to vote for its party at the next election. At election time, political parties are given time on radio and television to get their message across, but they are not allowed advertising time as they are in the USA.

Many organisations reach their audience via Facebook and Twitter. These both have the advantage of being free.

You will explore ways in which groups, individuals and those in power use the media to influence public opinion.

Pressure and campaign groups

Pressure and campaign groups that have good access to the media are likely to have more influence than others. Some can afford to employ public relations companies to help them inform people about their objectives. They are likely to have a louder voice and sway people's opinions. The media itself can take up issues and campaign for change – as you saw on pages 134 and 135.

These images show how groups campaign and attract attention in order to achieve their objectives. WWF works to look after the environment. Amnesty helps people who are under threat.

Action

If you had an issue that you wanted to get sorted out, how would you make a start in your local area?

Another point of view

'The government shouldn't waste money telling us about its work.'

Individuals

Individuals sometimes take up an issue, particularly when a member of their family or a friend has had to face a challenge. They will often start with the local media – the newspaper, radio or TV.

Making change happen ....

When Julie Bailey's mother died in North Staffordshire Hospital, she knew she hadn't been treated properly. She tried to raise the issues with the hospital but got no answer – so she wrote to the local paper. Letters flooded in as a result and she realised that she was not alone. 'Cure the NHS' was formed. The group's actions resulted in a public enquiry into the care provided by the hospital. After the enquiry, there was much change at the hospital.

Check your understanding

1 What is public opinion?

2 What are the main influences on public opinion?

3 What is the role of the media in forming public opinion?

4 Why does the government want to persuade people that its policies are working?

5 Why do pressure groups want to put issues that they support in front of as many people as possible?

6 Why do you think individuals resort to the media when they face a problem they can't sort out?

7 Why do you think some organisations have more impact than others?

Getting you thinking

Citizens of the European Union

Any citizen of a country within the European Union (EU) is automatically an EU citizen. This does not interfere with your national rights but adds four special rights to them:

- freedom to move and take up residence anywhere in the EU
- the right to vote and stand in local government and European Parliament elections in the country where you live
- an EU representative to help you out if you are in difficulties wherever you are in the world
- if you feel that EU rulings have not been carried out properly the right to appeal to the European ombudsman to investigate.

1 What advantages does being a member of the European Union have for UK Citizens?

2 Are there any disadvantages to the UK of EU membership?

Ken Tatham, an Englishman, became mayor of his village in France.

What is the EU?

At the end of the Second World War in 1945, the countries of Europe were anxious that war should not break out again. By joining together more closely, they felt that war would be less likely. Ever since 1958, more countries have become involved and have worked together more closely in all sorts of areas, including economics, politics, the environment and social issues.

The European Union:

- promotes economic and social progress
- has a voice on the international scene
- introduces EU citizenship
- develops an area of freedom, security and justice
- maintains and establishes EU regulations.

EU member countries
Countries applying for EU membership

Iceland
Sweden
Finland
Norway
Estonia
Latvia
Ireland
Denmark
Lithuania
United Kingdom
Netherlands
Germany
Poland
Belgium
Luxembourg
Czech Republic
Slovakia
France
Austria
Hungary
Switzerland
Slovenia
Croatia
Romania
Bosnia
Serbia
Bulgaria
Portugal
Italy
Montenegro
Spain
Macedonia
Albania
Turkey
Greece
Cyprus
Malta

How the EU works

All member countries, or **member states**, of the EU elect Members of the European Parliament (MEPs). MEPs have much bigger constituencies than MPs in each country because the European Parliament has to represent all the member countries: more than 500 million people in total.

The European Parliament has 751 members altogether.

The European Parliament is one of the five organisations that run the EU. It is, however, not quite like the UK Parliament, which has the power to make laws. Look at the diagram below to decide where the power lies.

Where does the power lie?

The European Commission

- Proposes new regulations
- Makes sure EU regulations are carried out
- Oversees the EU administration

The Court of Justice

- Decides whether European regulations have been broken

The European Parliament

- Discusses proposals for new regulations put forward by the European Commission
- Enforces EU regulations
- Can call for new policies to be launched and for existing ones to be changed

The Court of Auditors

- Checks that EU money has been spent properly

The Council of Ministers

- Is the main decision-making body
- Is made up of one minister from each member state
- Discusses proposals for new regulations put forward by the European Commission

Council of Europe – European Union: what's the difference?

Council of Europe	European Union (EU)
The Council of Europe has 47 member states.	The EU has 28 member states.
It aims to develop and spread the awareness of human rights to its members. It has developed the European Convention on Human Rights and organised the European Court of Human Rights.	It aims to promote economic and social progress by developing a group that can trade freely with each other. Members must obey the rules passed by the EU.
The Council of Europe requires its members to maintain its good standing of democracy and human rights.	European Union members must keep their economies running smoothly as this affects all the other member states.

Check your understanding

1 What are the organisations that run the EU?

2 Which organisation in the EU holds most power?

3 How is the EU different from the UK in this respect?

4 How democratic is decision making in the EU compared with the UK?

Another point of view

'Countries that trade together should all have the same rules for running businesses.'

Action

1 Which European constituency are you in?

2 Who is your MEP?

3 Which political party does your MEP belong to?

Key terms

member state: a country that is a member of the EU

Getting you thinking

Fish catches in Europe are limited to preserve fish stocks.

The European Union (EU) is a trading area. When countries sell things to each other, taxes often have to be paid on products before they are allowed into the other country. The EU removed these taxes between countries within the EU so that they could trade freely with each other.

In order to allow this trade to be as free as possible, rules have been drawn up about a range of things that affect the way businesses work. The rules aim to make competition fairer between countries, so they are all working on 'a level playing field'.

The rules are about:

Protecting employees

Without EU regulations, one country could allow children to work in factories. That country could make things more cheaply because wages would be lower.

Protecting the environment

If one country allowed businesses to pollute the environment, production would be cheaper because they wouldn't have to clean up the mess that was made.

Guaranteeing product standards

If a country is making poor-quality products, they may be dangerous.

Promoting fair competition

Businesses are not allowed to have too much power. For example, if a business controlled prices unfairly, this would hurt the customer.

1 Why do you think the EU has rules like this?

2 If one country broke the rules, how might this affect other countries in the EU?

3 Why is it necessary to have rules for all European countries about things like fishing?

4 What other things do you think Europe should have rules about?

Inside or out?

The EU has a population of around 500 million people – more than the US and Japan put together. This makes one very big market for businesses to sell to. It also means there is lots of competition, so prices should be lower.

The downside is that things bought from countries outside the EU are more expensive. A tax, or **customs duty**, has to be paid on goods from other parts of the world, so these goods would probably cost more for an EU consumer. These factors have meant that the UK buys more products from and sells more products to EU countries than any other part of the world.

The EU has its own laws, ranging from human rights to the environment and working conditions. Belonging to a member state, people in the UK have to abide by them. 'Getting you thinking' gives you some ideas about the sort of laws that exist.

One of the benefits of the EU is that it gives support to countries to develop infrastructure. This mean financial help to build new roads and various sorts of support for communities.

EUROPEAN UNION
EUROPEAN REGIONAL
DEVELOPMENT FUND

You will investigate how people and organisations in the UK are affected by European Union regulations.

Here is an example.

Gainsborough Square, Bristol

Gainsborough Square is a very run-down site on a housing estate in Bristol. The EU is putting money in to help Bristol council develop the area to provide a community hub. It will have a children's play centre and spaces to run courses to help people find work. The EU has given about £500 000 towards the project

Gainsborough Square

A bigger market

Roy Stewart turned his hobby into a business when he developed remote-controlled golf bags. At first he thought he would just sell to the UK market through his internet site. Once on the web, he found that he had started to trade internationally. He now has a growing business in both the UK and Europe. There is lots of competition in the golf market so Roy must keep his costs down and his prices competitive.

When he sells to countries in the EU there are no taxes to pay. An American company selling to the EU would have to pay taxes on its products.

1 Do you think Roy Stewart thinks the EU is a good or a bad thing?

2 What advantages are there in making products in the UK rather than the USA, for example?

3 Why does Roy have to keep his cost down?

4 What effect does the EU have on the prices customers pay?

Check your understanding

1 Give two reasons why it can be cheaper to buy goods from within the EU than from outside it.

2 What sorts of EU laws affect life in the UK?

3 How are business affected by the EU?

Action

1 What does European citizenship mean to people who you know?

2 Would they describe themselves as Europeans? Are there any situations in which they would be more or less likely to call themselves Europeans?

Another point of view

'I am a European.'

Key terms   **customs duty:** taxes on products bought from other countries

Getting you thinking

Human rights is at the heart of the Commonwealth's values. To support the work of member countries' police forces, the Commonwealth has developed a programme of training in human rights. The programme covers all aspects from arresting people to dealing with vulnerable people.

'Most Commonwealth police officers would no doubt see themselves as servants of the public: as protectors, not violators, of human rights.'

Commonwealth grant supports 60 pupils in rural areas

When Abigail was just a child, both her parents died. Her elderly grandmother took her in, but Abigail could not afford to buy the clothes, the books or the stationery she needed to go to school. A £20 000 grant from the Commonwealth Secretariat is supporting 60 young women like Abigail to continue their education at rural schools in Zambia. Poverty makes it difficult for girls in rural Africa to stay in school and gain qualifications, which in turn makes it harder for them to find employment to break out of the cycle of poverty.

'When I start working, I want to help other orphaned children and put them through school. Teaching a girl is a very beautiful thing,' she says.

1 Why do police need to be trained in human rights?

2 What difference does this make to the way a country runs?

3 How has the Commonwealth helped Abigail?

4 How has the Commonwealth helped Zambia by helping Abigail?

The Commonwealth today

The **Commonwealth of Nations**, usually just called the Commonwealth, is an association of countries, most of which were ruled by Britain. However, today's Commonwealth is a world away from the handful of countries that were the first members. From Africa and Asia to the Pacific and the Caribbean, the Commonwealth's two billion people make up 30 per cent of the world's population.

The modern Commonwealth helps to advance democracy, human rights, sustainable economic and social development within its member countries and beyond. Zimbabwe was thrown out of the Commonwealth in 2003 because it infringed human rights and its elections were not very democratic. All the countries have English as a common working language and similar systems of law, public administration and education. The Queen, like her predecessors, is head of the Commonwealth. It has built on its shared history to become a vibrant and growing association of states.

How does it do its work?

The Commonwealth has all sorts of ways of helping people and encouraging them to work together. Read about two examples on the page opposite.

Intro banner: *You will find out how the Commonwealth has changed from its origins, and the type of work it does today.*

Commonwealth members

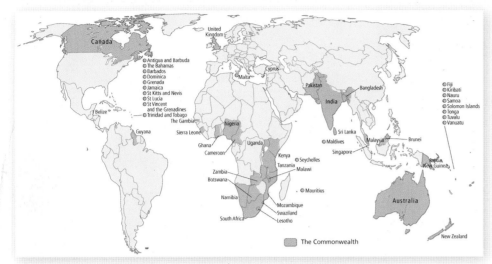

The Commonwealth Fund for Technical Cooperation promotes economic and social development, and helps to overcome poverty in member countries. The skills of member countries are used to help others. Advisors go to other countries to help in agriculture, enterprise, trade, legal issues, etc.

The Commonwealth Youth Credit Initiative (CYCI) is a small enterprise scheme for young people, providing **micro-credit**, training and enterprise development, which can bring economic self-sufficiency to the poorest young people. The CYCI uses the following methods:

- enables young people to support each other, and to encourage saving and the paying back of loans
- low interest rates
- low training costs
- ongoing training and monitoring of enterprises.

The Commonwealth's mission

All members must commit to the Commonwealth's mission

A platform for building global agreement

- It holds conferences that bring all the countries together to discuss major issues. This helps everyone to work together better.

A source of practical help for sustainable development

- The Commonwealth helps people to work so they can look after themselves, and has programmes that aim to look after the environment.

A force for making democracy work

- The Commonwealth helps its members to develop working democracy. It sends observers to check that elections are carried out properly.

Action

1 Have any countries joined the Commonwealth recently?
2 What are the conditions for joining the Commonwealth?
3 Why do countries want to be members of the Commonwealth?
4 Find an example of a recent Commonwealth sustainable development programme and present your findings to the class.

Check your understanding

1 What are the origins of the Commonwealth?
2 How has it changed over the years?
3 What is its mission today?
4 Describe some ways in which it achieves its mission.

Another point of view

'The Commonwealth is the same as it has always been.'

Key terms

Commonwealth of Nations: a voluntary group of independent countries
micro-credit: making small loans to individuals to help them help themselves

Getting you thinking

UNICEF

Thirteen-year-old Zahra has fled bombing, killings and chaos in Syria – but she says the worst thing has been losing her education. Her school in Aleppo was destroyed. Her family abandoned their home and fled to Lebanon. They live in a refugee camp in Lebanon. Zahra dreams of becoming a doctor but has missed so much education.

Going to class gives a sense of routine and normality amidst the chaos of life as a refugee. For refugee children, being in school offers a safe space to remember that they are children, to feel hope for the future, to play and to begin the process of healing.

Zahra has joined specialist catch-up classes run by a UNICEF partner organisation to try to help her gain a place in a mainstream school in Lebanon. She should not lose her dream.

1. How has UNICEF helped individual students like Zahra?
2. How has this project helped children in refugee camps?
3. Why does the UN spend money on projects like this?

The aims of the United Nations

Nearly every nation in the world belongs to the United Nations. Its membership totals 192 countries. When states join, they agree to accept the UN charter. The aims of the charter are:

- to maintain international peace and security
- to develop friendly relations among nations
- to cooperate in solving international problems and in promoting respect for human rights
- to be a centre for harmonising the actions of nations.

The UN is not a world government and it does not make laws. It does, however, help to resolve international conflict and makes policies on matters affecting us all. At the UN, all the member states have a voice and can vote in this process.

The organisation of the UN

The UN's General Assembly is made up of representatives of all the member countries. Each country has one vote. The Assembly makes recommendations, which are approved by the Security Council and put into action by the Secretary General. You will find out more about the legal aspects of the UN later on (see pages 152–3).

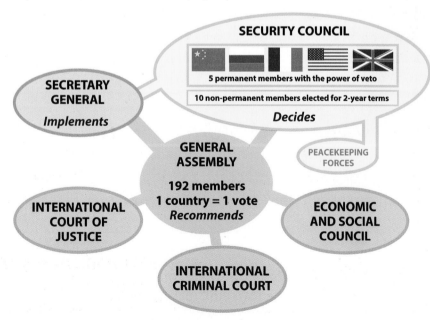

SECURITY COUNCIL

5 permanent members with the power of veto

10 non-permanent members elected for 2-year terms

Decides

SECRETARY GENERAL
Implements

PEACEKEEPING FORCES

GENERAL ASSEMBLY
192 members
1 country = 1 vote
Recommends

INTERNATIONAL COURT OF JUSTICE

ECONOMIC AND SOCIAL COUNCIL

INTERNATIONAL CRIMINAL COURT

The agencies

The UN has agencies that deal with the whole range of human and economic development, including the environment, population, food and agriculture, health and tourism. They carry out the activities agreed by the General Assembly and the Security Council. Here are just a few of them.

UNDP	United Nations Development Programme
UNIFEM	United Nations Development Fund for Women
UNHCR	Office of the United Nations High Commissioner for Refugees
UNICEF	United Nations Children's Fund
UNESCO	United Nations Educational, Scientific and Cultural Organisation
WB	World Bank
IMF	International Monetary Fund

Peacekeeping: the work of the UN Security Council

The Security Council is made up of five permanent members, including the United Kingdom, and 15 non-permanent members who are elected for two years at a time. As the world changes, the number of permanent members may change. The Security Council:

- can investigate any international dispute
- can recommend ways of reaching a settlement
- is responsible for peacekeeping forces.

You will find out more on page 146.

Action

1 Check how countries are progressing to achieve the Sustainable Development Goals.
2 Which agencies are likely to be useful in achieving the goals? Explain how.
3 Make a presentation to others explaining the goals and how the UN is helping to achieve them.

Check your understanding

1 What is the UN?
2 Who are the members?
3 Explain the structure and responsibilities of the main organisations of the UN.
4 Why did the UN set up the Millennium and Sustainable Development Goals?
5 Which agencies will help countries to achieve them?

Another point of view

'There are too many challenges for the UN to be any use.'

The Sustainable Development Goals 2015

In 2000, the UN set up the Millennium Development Goals. They aimed to improve life in the developing world by the year 2015. Much progress was made, but there was still further to go. In 2015, the Sustainable Development Goals were put in place.

End poverty

End hunger

Ensure good health and wellbeing

Ensure education for all

Gender equality

Ensure clean water and sanitation

Ensure affordable clean energy

Promote industry, innovation and infrastructure

Reduce inequalities

Make cities and communities sustainable

Ensure sustainable consumption and production

Combat climate change and its impacts

Conserve and sustainably use seas and oceans

Protect, restore and sustainably use the land

Promote peace, justice and strong institutions

4.20 The UN at work

Getting you thinking

A Swedish soldier helps the returning refugees.

When civil war broke out in Liberia, 340,000 people fled in fear. Once peace was established, the United Nations refugee agency began to bring them home.

The United Nations High Commission for Refugees also worked with communities to rehabilitate and construct schools, water and sanitation systems, shelter, bridges and roads, which were all severely damaged during the 14-year conflict.

1 Why do you think people left Liberia?

2 Why do you think refugees needed help to return home?

3 How did the UN help Liberian communities?

4 Why do you think people respect the soldiers from the UN?

A country's role

Keeping the peace throughout the world is one of the aims of the United Nations. When war breaks out and people are suffering, the UN's Security Council discusses what to do. There is a long list of issues and resolutions, as they call the decisions, every year.

Member countries benefit from being part of a worldwide organisation that wants to protect human rights and keep the peace. As part of membership, countries promise to provide troops, if called upon, to deal with peace keeping across the world. The UK has recently sent troops to join UN activities in the Democratic Republic of Congo, Cyprus and Sudan.

A member also contributes to the UN's budget. The aim is to make sure that the organisation is not dependent on one country. The amount depends on the wealth of the country, so richer countries contribute more than poorer ones.

The Members of the Security Council

There are five permanent members of the Security Council and 10 elected members who serve for two years. All representatives must be in New York, where the Security Council is based, all the time to deal with emergencies.

The permanent members

France   UK   USA   China   Russia

The elected members

Africa	3 members
Asia	2 members
Western Europe and 'Others'	2 members
Eastern Europe	1 member
Latin America and the Caribbean	2 members

You will investigate the ways the United Nations carries out its peacekeeping and humanitarian work.

Humanitarian action and human rights

People throughout the world are deprived of their human rights when war breaks out. As in Liberia, UN troops, who come from member countries, are sent in to help solve the problems.

Refugees

For more than five decades, the United Nations High Commission on Refugees has been helping the world's uprooted people.

The agency's first task was to help an estimated one million people after World War II. During the 1950s, the refugee crisis spread to Africa, Asia and then back to Europe. It had become a global problem.

During its lifetime, the agency has assisted an estimated 50 million refugees to restart their lives.

Action

1 Research a current UN peacekeeping operation. Why are people fighting? How is the UN helping? Is it 'maintaining international peace and security'?

2 Find a recent example of work done by the UN High Commission on Refugees. Why had the refugees left home? How has the High Commission helped?

Check your understanding

1 What kind of work does the UN do?

2 Is the UN a government? Explain your answer.

3 Describe the Security Council's responsibilities.

4 Why is the UK important in the Security Council?

5 Why do you think the UN needs to intervene in the conflicts mentioned?

6 Why might the UN be able to help refugees more effectively than individual countries?

7 Which human rights are the child soldiers being denied?

Child soldiers

Child soldiers in Africa are often looked after by the UN and educated in order to fit into society again. Often their families can't be found. This is just one of many projects to help people in difficulties.

'The soldiers gave me training. They gave me a gun. I took drugs. I killed civilians. Lots. It was just war, what I did then. I only took orders. I knew it was bad. It was not my wish.'

A former child soldier being helped at a rehabilitation centre

Drawing by a former child soldier of the armed group, National Liberation Forces, Burundi, 2006.

Another point of view

'Countries should not be allowed to be members of the UN if their populations' human rights are not respected.'

147

Getting you thinking

Resolute Support

Once soldiers were pulled out of Afghanistan, a NATO-led mission called Resolute Support was launched to provide training, advice and assistance to the Afghan security forces and institutions.

It included 12,000 personnel from both NATO and partner nations.

It will help the army to:

- recruit, train, manage and develop its personnel
- plan, organise and budget
- ensure that it is accountable for its activities
- ensure that it accepts the rule of law.

What is NATO?

NATO stands for The North Atlantic Treaty Organisation. It was set up after the Second World War so the countries around the North Atlantic could protect themselves. This statement comes from the agreement and sets out the relationship.

> *an armed attack upon one...shall be considered an attack upon them all.*

1 Why do you think the Afghan army needed support?

2 Why should other countries want to help?

NATO's aim is to ensure the freedom and security of its members through political and military means.

Political

NATO promotes democratic values and encourages consultation and cooperation on defence and security issues to build trust and, in the long run, prevent conflict.

Military

NATO is committed to the peaceful resolution of disputes. If diplomatic efforts fail, it has the military capacity needed to undertake crisis-management operations, alone or in cooperation with other countries and international organisations.

You will explore NATO and the benefits and obligations that come with the UK's membership.

4.21 NATO: what it is and what it does

NATO members

Albania, Belgium, Bulgaria, Canada, Croatia, Czech Republic, Denmark, Estonia, France, Germany, Greece, Hungary, Iceland, Italy, Latvia, Lithuania, Luxembourg, Netherlands, Norway, Poland, Portugal, Romania, Slovakia, Slovenia, Spain, Turkey, The United Kingdom, The United States

The Work of NATO

Until the terrorist attacks on The World Trade Center in New York, NATO defended national borders. After these 9/11 attacks, it joined the war on terrorism.

NATO says that 'Peacekeeping has become at least as difficult as peacemaking.'

As a result, NATO is developing strong bonds with countries across the world and working in ways that are not just military.

The UK's role

The UK has a delegation, or group of representatives, who keep the government in touch with NATO's plans and discussions.

It contributes to NATO's budget and keeps up defence spending at home to make sure that it can support NATO when required.

Michael Fallon, the Secretary of State for Defence, announced in Parliament that the UK will contribute 3000 personnel to the Very High Readiness Joint Task Force from 2016.

It is made up of sea, land and air units, which will serve as a 'Spearhead force' to respond at short notice to any threat to NATO.

British, US and Dutch troops on a joint exercise

Action

Find out about any NATO missions that involve the UK at the moment.

Check your understanding

1 What does NATO stand for?

2 What does NATO aim to do?

3 How does it support the UK?

4 What are the UK's responsibilities as a member of NATO?

Another point of view

'Nations should be able to defend themselves, not rely on the help of others.'

Key terms

NATO: the North Atlantic Treaty Organisation, whose members work together to defend each other

Getting you thinking

1 Make a list of things that these young people might have have bought recently.

2 Where do you think they have come from? Check the labels on your clothes and other stuff to give you some ideas.

3 When you go shopping, what is most important about the price of things you buy?

4 Can you make any connections between where things come from and the price you paid?

What does the World Trade Organization do?

Trade is a very important way for any country to earn money and create jobs. People and countries have traded for thousands of years, but in today's global economy, information, goods and money can be moved around the world at an incredible speed. Companies aim to make the best product at the cheapest price. As you saw in 'Getting you thinking', people usually want to buy things as cheaply as possible.

The World Trade Organization (WTO) is responsible for negotiating international trade agreements. Its objective is to make trade as free as possible. This means that one country should not charge taxes, or **tariffs**, when they buy things from another country. As a member, a country's commitment is to keep the rules.

When countries disagree, the WTO will help to sort out the dispute. If a country is charging tariffs when it shouldn't, or limiting the amount of a product that it will import from another country, the WTO will look at the issue and come to a decision about who is right and wrong.

You will find out about the role of the World Trade Organization and the UK's commitments and benefits.

4.22 The World Trade Organization

Free trade or fair trade

Most rich countries want a **free trade** system in which the prices of goods are determined by the amount that people want to buy and sell.

However, many people believe such a system favours richer countries, such as the USA and Japan, and want the WTO to be reformed. They argue that world trade must be managed so the poorest countries benefit more. In other words, they want world trade to become fair trade. Fair trade is trade that is good for the producer; the **Fair Trade** system has been set up to ensure that more of the price consumers pay goes to the producer. Fair Trade staff will be paid a fair wage, have good working conditions and be allowed to form trade unions to defend their rights.

Fair Trade campaigns, such as the Clean Clothes Campaign (CCC), have drawn attention to the working conditions of workers all around the world.

The Clean Clothes Campaign code for garments workers ensures:

- freedom to join a trade union
- no discrimination
- no forced or slave labour
- health and safety checks
- 48 hours maximum working week
- a fair wage.

Action

1 Use the internet to research UK companies trying to promote Fair Trade.

2 Obtain details of company 'codes' like the CCC code above. Use these to create a leaflet or poster explaining the issues about Fair Trade and its aims for helping workers in less economically developed countries. You could run an assembly to explain Fair Trade to the rest of your school.

Check your understanding

1 In your own words, say what the World Trade Organisation (WTO) does.

2 Why do some people want to reform the WTO?

3 How would Fair Trade help workers in less economically developed countries?

4 What human rights do groups such as the Clean Clothes Campaign help to protect?

To buy or not to buy

The Clean Clothes Campaign does not think consumers should **boycott** goods that are not 'clean', because it believes boycotts will put employees out of work. When the US government talked about bringing in a law to stop anything made by children under 15 from being imported to the USA, many child employees in Bangladesh were thrown out of work and their families often went hungry as a result.

Another point of view

'People in the UK should boycott companies that sell "dirty" clothes and trainers.'

Key terms

boycott: to refuse to use or have anything to do with something

Fair Trade: a system of buying and selling products that aims to pay the producer a fair price

free trade: trade between countries which is not restricted by things like high taxes on imports

tariffs: taxes to be paid on a some imports or exports

Humanitarian horror

Hundreds of fighters, including children under the age of 15, attacked Bogoro – a village in the Democratic Republic of Congo. They were armed with semiautomatic weapons, rocket-propelled grenades and knives. The soldiers circled the village and converged towards the centre, killing at least 200 civilians and imprisoning survivors in a room filled with corpses. Some residents of the village were killed when their houses were set on fire and others were hacked to death with machetes.

The two suspects, Germain Katanga and Mathieu Ngudjolo Chui were charged with six counts of war crimes and three counts of crimes against humanity, relating to the attack on the village of Bogoro. One was sent to prison for 12 years. The other was released because of lack of evidence.

1 Which human rights did the fighters deprive people of?

2 Why do you think the Congolese authorities handed the men over to the court?

The International Criminal Court

The International Criminal Court was set up in 2002. It is entirely independent but was born out of the United Nations, which can refer issues to the court.

Over 100 countries have signed up and more are committed to joining. However, some important countries have refused to join because they are critical of the court. These include USA, China, Russia and India.

The court only deals with the most serious crimes, including **genocide**, crimes against humanity and war crimes.

The court is a 'last resort', as it will not deal with cases that countries are dealing with themselves. It will, however, take on cases if a country is holding a trial but is really protecting the offenders.

If the court is going to be understood by the people in the countries affected by its activities, it must communicate with the local people. In the Congo, for example, it has used TV docudramas and interactive radio programmes in local languages as well as holding discussions with ethnic communities.

What law?

For a court to make rulings, it needs laws on which to base its decisions. The **Geneva Convention** sets out the rules for how people should be treated in war. Most countries have signed up to it. There have been some additional rules since the Convention was set up in 1949. These include rules related to the use of biological and chemical weapons and anti-personnel mines.

The Geneva Convention

1 People who are not involved in hostilities must be protected and treated humanely.

2 It is forbidden to kill or injure an enemy who surrenders.

3 The wounded and sick shall be collected and cared for by the people which has them in its power.

4 Captured combatants and civilians are entitled to respect for their lives, dignity, personal rights and convictions. They shall have the right to correspond with their families and to receive relief.

5 No one shall be held responsible for an act he has not committed. No one shall be subjected to physical or mental torture, corporal punishment or cruel or degrading treatment.

6 It is prohibited to employ weapons or methods of warfare of a nature to cause unnecessary losses or excessive suffering.

7 The civilian population must not be attacked. Attacks shall be directed solely against military objectives.

Action

1 What conflicts are going on in the world today?

2 Find out how people's human rights are affected.

3 Has the UN's Security Council expressed a view?

4 Has anyone been referred to the International Criminal Court?

5 Find out about the trials that are going on.

Not to be confused with …

The International Court of Justice, which is a UN organisation. Its objective is to settle disputes between member countries. It was asked to rule on the West Bank Barrier, which Israel claimed it had built to protect the country from terrorism. The opposition to it claimed that Israel was taking land that wasn't theirs and preventing Palestinians from moving freely in the area – including going to work. The International Court of Justice ruled that the wall was illegal. Israel rejected the ruling and the wall is still there.

The West Bank Barrier

Another point of view

'Countries should be left to sort out their own humanitarian criminals.'

Check your understanding

1 How was the International Criminal Court set up?

2 What issues does it deal with?

3 Which countries have refused to join?

4 How does it try to explain its activities to local people?

5 What rules does the Geneva Convention set out?

6 What does the International Court of Justice do?

Key terms

Geneva Convention: an internationally accepted set of rules on the treatment of people in war

genocide: mass murder of a racial, national or religious group

Getting you thinking

Collective action

A squalid refugee camp in Ghana was home to hundreds of child soldiers and refugees, many of whom had fled from Liberia. Mediators Beyond Borders, a charity, was training a group of them in practical skills as well as offering help with anger management and counselling.

Pump Aid is a charity that aims to bring clean water and sanitation to Liberia, one of the poorest countries in the world. The trainees from the refugee camp offered the basic skills and the enthusiasm to help. Cynthia and Benjamin, now in their twenties, were two of the first ex-child soldiers to be employed by Pump Aid. They assess the needs of places and install the pumps. In a country where there is 85 per cent unemployment, the security of a job makes life very different.

1 Who has helped these young people?

2 How have they been helped?

3 How are they helping others?

4 How are the charities supporting people's human rights?

5 Why do you think that charities can find it easier than government organisations to work in areas like this?

The work of non-governmental organisations

Helping to develop

Non-governmental organisations, or NGOs, aim to help people in difficulties. They may be refugees, people living in places where there are natural disasters or those who need help to move out of poverty.

In 'Getting you thinking' you learned about two NGOs which help development in different ways. One gave practical help with clean water; the other provided education so there was the prospect of a job for the children who had been child soldiers.

All this support is improving people's human rights. These examples are the right to education and the right to food and water.

Many NGOs are charities and depend on donations to carry out their work. If you look at the websites of Mediators Beyond Borders and Pump Aid, you will see that they are both looking for donations. They are drawing on public support to have greater impact.

You will learn how non-governmental organisations can give relief and help development.

4.24 Who can help?

ShelterBox

ShelterBox provide emergency shelter and vital supplies to support communities coping with disaster and humanitarian crisis around the world.

A ShelterBox is made to meet the needs of each emergency. It might contain heavy-duty sheeting and tools to help people rebuild their homes. For those who have lost everything, there are tents, cooking utensils, mosquito nets and water purification equipment.

To help keep life normal for children in these situations, there are SchoolBoxes with everything necessary for 50 children.

The contents of a ShelterBox

Helping in crisis

Across the world there are frequent disasters. They may result from the weather, earthquakes, volcanoes and all sorts of other problems. People are often left with nothing. Their homes have been destroyed. They have no shelter, food or water. War can mean that people have to leave home in order to find somewhere safe to live. They often end up in a refugee camp where at least they are safe, but the living conditions can be dreadful.

Although these events hit the headlines for a short time, the effects last much longer. Many NGOs, like ShelterBox, step in immediately to provide shelter or food. Some NGOs go on giving help for as long as it is needed. UNICEF, an agency of the United Nations, supports people whose lives have been shattered by natural disasters or war, and continue to support people in refugee camps and those who need to rebuild their lives.

Many NGOs work across both types of help. UNICEF, for example, provides both emergency help as well as development help.

Action

What crises are there in the world at the moment? Which NGOs are helping? What are they doing?

Another point of view

'Governments should pay for the help given by NGOs.'

Check your understanding

1 What is an NGO?
2 What do NGOs do in crisis situations?
3 What do they do to help development?
4 Where do many get the money to pay for their activities?

Key terms

non-governmental organisations: organisations, not run by government, that support people in need of help

Getting you thinking

Helping ex-soldiers back into civilian life in Nepal.

Supporting 800 000 children back into education in northern Nigeria.

Sorting out 500 km of roads in Nepal.

Saving drinking water for 800 000 people in Sudan.

Creating 45 000 jobs in Somalia.

Nailatu Al-Quasm, 12, is one of the many girls who were enrolled at Gyezmo primary school by the Girls' Education Project. Nailaiu hopes to become a medical doctor when she grows up.

1 These are all places where there is conflict. The British government has been giving aid to help the countries in these ways. How do you think this aid will help to avoid conflict in each country?

2 Why do you think it might be better to prevent conflict in this way than try to stop it once it has started?

What is conflict?

When fighting breaks out in any country, the costs can be enormous.

People are killed.

Security, justice and state services are all affected.

Women and girls suffer violence.

People become refugees.

Trade links are cut so countries cannot buy and sell things.

Organised crime groups and terrorists move about more easily.

Recovery time is long once the war is over.

The cost to countries that try to stop the war by force is high as people die and equipment is lost.

It is much better to prevent war happening than to pay the costs – both human and financial – of letting it happen. There are times when people are being hurt and their human rights are under threat and other countries feel they must protect them. This means stepping in by using one of the means outlined on the next page.

What can be done?

Mediation

By bringing the two sides together to talk, war may be avoided. People who are respected by both sides can help to mediate. They must be seen not to support one side or the other. Today, more and more potential conflicts, or those in the early stages, are being settled by mediation and negotiation.

If it is to work, all parties must be involved. There is often more than one side and if they are not all listened to, any agreement will not work.

Another mediation strategy is to work through local organisations. The UK government has done this in West Africa, where it has supported The Economic Community for West African States. It has mediated, prevented several conflicts and negotiated a ceasefire agreement in this region. It has also helped after a war by developing peace-building programmes. These include improving the free movement of people and trade, and tackling both drugs and people trafficking.

Sanctions

Sanctions are put in place when the government does not approve of the actions of another country. Sanctions used to be placed on all sorts of things that ordinary people needed. This hurt people who were not involved so instead, sanctions are now targeted and often put on individual people.

All sanctions and embargoes are targeted. A 'targeted' restriction is focused on individual people or organisations. In some cases, a comprehensive restriction is put in place against a particular country's regime.

Examples of sanctions

- Bans on military equipment and support
- Financial sanctions on governments or individuals
- Travel bans on named people
- Bans on a range of raw materials and other products
- Bans on importing from a particular country

Force

If all else fails, the only solution may be to use force to stop two sides fighting. When people's human rights are being affected, the UK has had to step in.

This does not always mean fighting directly, but can involve supporting another country's army, often with training. You saw, when looking at the work of NATO, how important this can be.

The RAF may be used to police airspace if there is fear that the air force of another country is getting too close.

In the 21st century, UK forces have been sent to Kosovo, Sierra Leone, Afghanistan and Iraq.

A UK plane intercepts a foreign plane that is too close to another country's airspace.

Check your understanding

1 Why is conflict damaging?

2 How can conflict be prevented?

3 Why do you think improving people's lives makes them less likely to be involved in conflict?

4 What does mediation mean and how does it work best?

5 What are sanctions and why are they imposed?

6 Why are sanctions against whole nations not used so much now?

7 Why do you think sanctions might prevent conflict?

8 When might force be used?

Action

Find out about countries or people that the UK government has imposed sanctions on. What is the reason for the sanction? What is happening in the country concerned at the moment?

Another point of view

'Conflict is too expensive. The UK should not get involved.'

Key terms

sanction: a penalty for breaking rules, especially in international situations

Source A

In the wrong

The *Daily Express* claimed that the English language is dying out in schools. A complaint was made to the Independent Press Standards Organisation (IPSO) because the claim was inaccurate. The paper was ordered to place a correction on its front page because its claim was found to be inaccurate.

The paper said it had used official figures to support the claim. It had, however, used data that said that 311 languages were spoken in schools to claim that English-speaking pupils were 'becoming a minority in hundreds of classrooms'.

It also claimed that in some schools English was 'hardly heard at all' and that there were those in which 'foreign languages had overtaken English'.

It blamed a 'decades-long open door policy on immigration' for the situation.

IPSO ruled that the paper had 'distorted' the figures, which did not support its story,

The data showed the number of pupils whose first language was not English and did not record how many were unable to speak it at all. However, many children spoke their mother tongue as well as English so it did not measure the fall in the use of English in the country's schools.

IPSO's judgement said that the paper had caused damage because the claims were 'repeated throughout the entire article, including prominently in print in the front-page sub-headline, and because they were central to the report, on a matter of significant public importance'.

The *Daily Express* accepted that it 'may have suggested inaccurately that pupils who did not speak English as a first language could not speak English at all, and that English is not spoken in some classrooms'.

1. The source discusses the role of the Independent Press Standards Organisation. Using the source, explain the role of this organisation and why it is important. *(4 marks)*

    Role: The Independent Press Standards Organisation regulates newspapers. It deals with complaints when people feel that the Editors' Code of Practice has been broken. This was used to correct the actions of the Daily Express.

    Importance: It is important because newspapers should keep to the standards that are laid down in the Editors' Code of Practice. If they do not, IPSO can punish them by making them give a public apology for their mistakes. The Daily Express was told to do this.

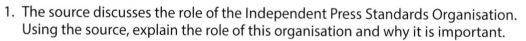

> The question says 'using the source', so it is important to do so if you want to get all the marks.

2. The *Daily Express* was trying to influence public opinion. Give one strength and one weakness of the method they used. *(2 marks)*

Strength: The paper has a large number of readers who will see its point of view.

Weakness: When they get it wrong, it may make people doubt what they say the rest of the time.

3. According to the source, the *Daily Express's* claims were:

    'repeated throughout the entire article, including prominently in print in the front-page sub-headline, … were central to the report, on a matter of significant public importance'.

Explain why IPSO found this to be damaging *(2 marks)*

The paper had made its point very strongly and told people, all through the article, things that are not true. The issue is important and it is not right for people to be misled in this way. It may make them believe things that are not true and make them more biased.

4. Explain why it is important for the press to be free and accurate. *(6 marks)*

If democracy is to work, the press must be free. If it is not, people will only be given the government's point of view. They will not know what is really going on so they will not be able to decide who to vote for. When the press is not free, the government is often not democratic. A government that restricts press freedom often restricts other freedoms so it is difficult for elections to be fair.

If it is not accurate it may mislead people, like the Daily Express was doing. If the press can say what it likes about people, it can again mislead people – so they believe things that are not true. It can also damage people who have not done anything. If newspapers tell stories about someone and it is not true, it will damage their reputation and it may be difficult to recover from. As people say, there is no smoke without fire.

If the press gives inaccurate information, it may hurt businesses, organisations and individuals. Even when the information in the press is accurate, sometimes sweeping statements are made. For instance, there has been a lot of newspaper coverage about charities pestering people for donations but not all charities do this. A paper must be accurate about things like this so other charities, for example, are not affected negatively.

The question asks the student to deal with freedom and accuracy. It is important to do both – but it doesn't have to be equal coverage.

Extended writing

'Well-organised protests always succeed in getting governments to think again.'
How far do you agree with this view?
Give reasons for your opinion, showing that you have considered other points of view.
In your answer, you could consider:
- protests by different groups of people
- how governments react to protest.

(15 marks)

A well-organised protest can bring about change because it explains the issues involved and puts forward a strong point of view. Sometimes governments haven't seen the side effects of their policies and when they are pointed out, they change to take these things into account.

> The student shows that they understand the issue and suggests a reason why protest might work.

To be well organised a protest will put forward information which sets out a clear case. It will also get publicity so many people hear about it and may decide to support the cause. It is useful to have the ear of people in positions of power so that they will take notice. Recently, Members of the House of Lords took up the case of people protesting about changes to tax credits – and went through the democratic process and the government had to change its plans. The people who are protesting also need to be well organised. Protesters who go out and do damage often put people off and hurt their cause. This has sometimes been the case with climate change protesters.

> Here the student deals with the 'well organised' part of the question.

Some organisations use dramatic measures to draw attention to their views. Greenpeace, for example, often does this. It has ships that block the way of boats carrying things or doing things they don't approve of. They protest against whaling, hoping to get the Japanese government to make their fishermen obey international rules. They have brought about some change but still think there is much more to do.

> The student is using good examples. You need to think about an example you know to support your answer.

Governments cannot always make the changes people want. Sometimes protesters are a minority so it would not be democratic to make changes – even when a protest is well organised. People often do not want wind turbines near them but the country needs renewable energy so the government ignores their protest. Sometimes they want more money spent on something and, as government funds are limited, not everyone can have everything they want. If it seems that the protesters do represent the majority, the government should listen. The government website where issues can be put forward is one way of recognising the views of the public and might be part of a well organised campaign. If more than 100 000 people sign up to a petition, there must be a debate in parliament.

In some countries protest is against the law. Protesters are sent to prison or worse when they try to tell the government that they do not like what it does. This happens in countries like China, North Korea and Zimbabwe.

The question says 'governments' so it is important to look beyond the UK.

I do not agree that well-organised protests always get governments to change their minds. A protest that is well organised is more likely to be effective but governments cannot always just change their policies and others never will. Just accepting the word of protesters is not very democratic as they may not represent the views of the majority.

The student has set out their point of view and drawn on their answer to support it.

Taking Citizenship action

5.1 Choosing your action

Getting you thinking

1 What issues do you think the young people in the picture might be discussing?

2 Think about your community – what needs changing?

3 What do you care about?

4 How do you think you can make a difference?

Young people in Devizes discuss community issues.

Questions to ask

Citizenship is all about joining in and having an effect. Citizenship action gives you the chance to have a go. There are lots of ways of participating, as you will have found out already.

There are many questions to ask before you decide on the issue you want to address.

What's the action?

You have a choice of two different types of action.

- Organise and deliver an event, meeting or campaign to persuade people about the cause you have chosen.

- Organise and deliver a project which will raise awareness and commitment and help other people.

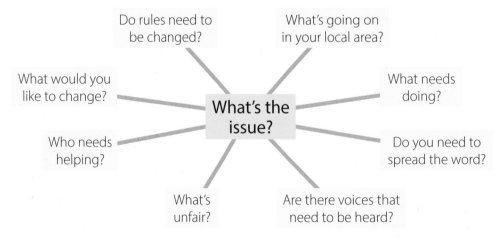

Do rules need to be changed?

What's going on in your local area?

What would you like to change?

What needs doing?

What's the issue?

Who needs helping?

Do you need to spread the word?

What's unfair?

Are there voices that need to be heard?

How does it fit into Citizenship?

Look back at the work you have done so far and work out where your chosen issue fits in with the content of the course. It is important to do this at the beginning so you can use the ideas in developing your action.

- Theme A: Living together in the UK
- Theme B: Democracy at work in the UK
- Theme C: How the law works
- Theme D: Power and influence

You will identify an issue, problem or social need for your action.

5.1 Choosing your action

What issue?

- Do you care about human rights? Who is being treated badly?
- Do you care about democracy? Who isn't having a say?
- Do you care about things being fair? Who isn't being treated as you think they should?
- Do you care about the law? Does something need to change?
- Do you care about the choices the government is making? What can you do about it?
- Do you care about the environment? What can you change?
- Is something going wrong in your community? Can you change it?
- Are people ill informed about our role in the world? Can you help?

Forming a team

In order to carry out your action, you need to be a member of a team – which means you need at least a partner, or probably a larger group. It might be a group of your friends, but you will need to make sure that the group has people with the range of expertise you need to carry out your action. Although you will all need to take part in each stage of the action, it's useful to have people who can lead on different aspects and take responsibility for carrying out each step.

A team needs to be made up of people with different skills. Think about who is good at:

- planning
- research
- organising
- communicating
- considering points of view
- negotiating
- advocacy.

Combining all these skills with help your action and you will help each other to develop the skills too.

Take action

Sit down with a blank sheet of paper and think about the Citizenship action you want to do.

1 Start by writing down all your ideas.
2 List all the advantages and disadvantages of each idea.
3 Put them in order from best to worst.
4 Is the one at the top the one you really want to carry out? If so, go ahead. If not, have another look at the list.

Checkpoints

Before you make a final decision, check with your teacher that your activity is suitable for the course requirements.

How to persuade

In Theme D, 'Power and influence', you learned about how individuals and organisations can influence and persuade people about their points of view (page 112 'Putting on the pressure'). You also explored ways that people use the media to get their message over (page 136 'People, pressure groups and the media').

When you are working out what you are going to do, you will need to think carefully about the sort of methods you will use to find out people's views and to persuade them of yours. You will find help a little later in the book to develop the skills you will need.

A voice in the community – young people in Stoke on Trent voting for their representatives

Care about Fair Trade? Run your own cooperative.

5.2 Carrying out research

Getting you thinking

1 What sort of research is being carried out by these students?

2 How will the information they are collecting be different?

3 Why would you use these different methods of research?

4 Think about the issue you have chosen and work out how these two types of research would help you to decide what to do.

What sort of research?

When you set up and plan your action, you will need to carry out different sorts of research.

First of all, you will need to carry out some **secondary research** to find out more about the topic you have selected. It might be an issue, problem, cause or social need.

Secondary research means using information that has been collected by other people. This might be:

- published sources of data
- findings and official reports from public bodies
- reports in the news and media
- information about NGOs, groups and other organisations
- opinion polls
- statistics
- videos.

The government and its agencies collect all sorts of data. In ' How the law works' (page 80) you saw how local crime data can tell you about what is happening in your local area. Often, NGOs and pressure groups will collect information and produce reports to support their cause. All these can contribute to your decisions on how to go about your action.

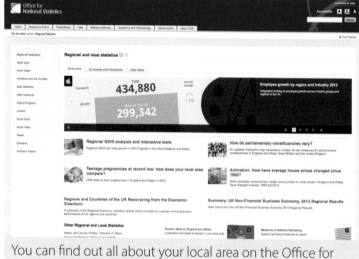

You can find out all about your local area on the Office for National Statistics website.

What are your research questions?

Research questions help you to plan your action and the research you need to do in order to decide how to carry it out.

Working together on a spider diagram to list the things you want to find out will help you decide what questions to ask. Once you have a list, put the questions in order so you can see a logical sequence for your work.

You will find out about using primary and secondary research in preparing for your action.

5.2 Carrying out research

Setting about your primary research

Once you have your research questions, you can decide how to get answers to them. You will probably need to carry out **primary research** to find out what people think about your issue.

There are a variety of different strategies you might use to find out people's views:

- observing or recording people to gather information
- discussing the issue with members of the community
- interviewing people to collect qualitative and quantitative data
- using polls, votes and surveys to gather data.

Putting together questionnaires and surveys requires some practice if you are to get useful information. You will find out more about this on page 168.

Summing up the evidence

While researching your issue, you will have found that people have different points of view. You will now need to weigh up all the evidence and decide why some people's views contribute more than others.

- If people are looking at the issue in a way that takes many people's needs into account, their views are more likely to be helpful. The views of those who think only about their own perspective probably won't be so useful.

- You will also need to be able to distinguish fact from opinion. The media can provide a great deal of evidence, but if it is biased it may not be very helpful.

- If the evidence has involved counting people's views it is **quantitative data**. Providing that this has been collected carefully, it can be very useful because it is 'hard evidence' of people's views or what is going on.

- **Qualitative data** involves gathering people's views and opinions. This has to be done carefully if you are going to be able to use it to compare different strategies.

Once you have considered all the evidence, the group needs to come to a conclusion about planning the action.

Take action

Once you have decided on the issue you want to deal with, sit down in a group and work out what you need to know about it. Think about where you can find the information and share out the research tasks. Fix a timeline so you can come together again to share your results and decide what to do next.

Checkpoints

When you decide on the action you are going to take, check with your teacher that you can achieve all the objectives of the Action and meet the exam requirements.

Key terms

primary research: new research to answer a particular question
qualitative data: deals with descriptions and cannot be counted
quantitative data: deals with information that can be counted or measured
secondary research: published research collected by other people

Getting you thinking

Should prisoners have the vote?

Yes they should!

'Prisoners should be allowed to vote because they are still part of society. When they come out, we want them to be responsible members of society. Okay, so they broke the law, but if they get to vote and give their opinion then they will feel that they are part of the community. I just think that it's not all that fair for some people to be excluded from voting. Also, human rights laws say that everyone has equal rights, so if we don't allow prisoners to vote, then we are breaking the law. No one is above the law in the UK.'

They gave up their right to vote!

'If a person chooses to commit a crime, they are branding themselves a criminal. Criminals should not be allowed to vote. It's as simple as that. Why should the leaders of a democracy be partly chosen by those who would seek to ruin and harm those around them? A democracy does not function as a democracy when the troublemakers are making the decisions.'

Would you take one of these points of view more seriously than the other? Explain why.

Why do people hold different points of view?

As you discovered in Theme A, 'Living together in the UK', we all have several identities. This means that we have different opinions about different things. Do you always agree with your friends and family? Start thinking about why you disagree. You will soon realise why there are issues that are difficult to deal with.

- Imagine you wanted to support the development of a new leisure centre – can you imagine why others might object?

- Imagine you wanted to support a particular charity – work out your reasons and think of reasons why your friends might want to support a different charity.

It is useful to think about other people's views before you discuss an issue with them. Keep a record of what is said in your discussions, as you will need this for group decision making.

I think …

but I think …

Are some opinions more valuable than others?

When you carry out your research, you will find all sorts of points of view – but you need to ask some questions about the quality of the ideas.

Questions to ask

Who runs the website? Sometimes it's hard to tell.

Do they have evidence to support their case?

Is it fact or just opinion?

Is the writer biased?

Do they have expertise?

What's the source of evidence?

Are they just self-interested?

Look at each question and work out how it affects the value of the evidence.

Weighing up the evidence

Once you have all the evidence, you will need to decide exactly what action to take. You will need to use all the questions to check your evidence and decide how useful it is in helping you to make decisions about how to move forward. The secondary research will generally set the direction for your action. The primary research will give you ideas about how to go about it.

Take action

When you have gathered all your evidence, sit down together and make a list of all the evidence that supports your case and another of evidence that doesn't. Work out what value you put on each piece of evidence and how it contributes to your case.

Checkpoints

Make sure that you have copies of the evidence and can explain how it helps you to decide on your action.

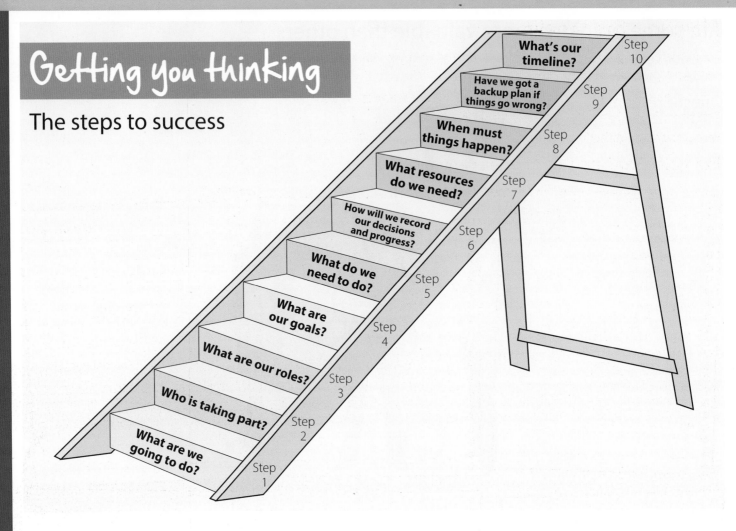

Getting you thinking

The steps to success

- **What's our timeline?** — Step 10
- **Have we got a backup plan if things go wrong?** — Step 9
- **When must things happen?** — Step 8
- **What resources do we need?** — Step 7
- **How will we record our decisions and progress?** — Step 6
- **What do we need to do?** — Step 5
- **What are our goals?** — Step 4
- **What are our roles?** — Step 3
- **Who is taking part?** — Step 2
- **What are we going to do?** — Step 1

Planning

Planning means setting out what must be done and making sure that everyone knows their responsibilities. By following the steps above, you will be on the right track. You will need to gather evidence and be able to explain the links to Citizenship, so you need to build this into your plan. The following pages will help you with the stages of organising your action and gathering the evidence you will need to know about all this for the exam.

What will you need to collect?

- Evidence to show why your issue is important locally and nationally
- An explanation of how it links to Citizenship
- Evidence that you have communicated with two people in positions of power or influence and found out what they thought
- An explanation of why people hold different points of view on your issue
- A description of how you can affect your issue through action

- Evidence of how you negotiated and decided on your action
- Evidence of your action
- Evidence of your contribution
- An assessment of the contribution of your action, locally and nationally
- Thoughts on whether your action has affected your views.

What will you need to do?

Brainstorm all the things that need to be done.

- Can you easily divide these things into groups?
- Who has the skills needed for each activity?
- Should people work in pairs or on their own?

When you have made these decisions, draw up a list to explain exactly what everyone has to do.

Make sure you keep the list safe. You will need it to check whether everything has been done and to put it in your records.

Planning the timeline

Look carefully at your plan and draw up a timeline, putting the name of the person responsible beside every point.

This will enable you to check whether everything is on track. It will also give everyone target dates for getting things done.

Remember that gathering information can take time, so make it a priority.

Example: Planning a Fair Trade event in school

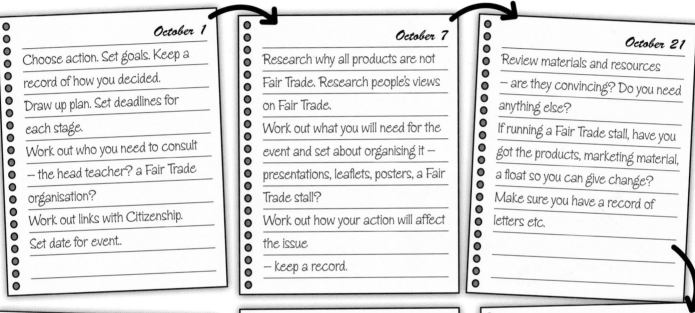

October 1
Choose action. Set goals. Keep a record of how you decided.
Draw up plan. Set deadlines for each stage.
Work out who you need to consult – the head teacher? a Fair Trade organisation?
Work out links with Citizenship.
Set date for event..

October 7
Research why all products are not Fair Trade. Research people's views on Fair Trade.
Work out what you will need for the event and set about organising it – presentations, leaflets, posters, a Fair Trade stall?
Work out how your action will affect the issue
– keep a record.

October 21
Review materials and resources – are they convincing? Do you need anything else?
If running a Fair Trade stall, have you got the products, marketing material, a float so you can give change?
Make sure you have a record of letters etc.

November 21
Review what happened.
Have you got enough evidence?
Do you need to find out more about whether you influenced people?
Work out how your action has affected the issue.
Work out whether it has affected your views.

November 14
The event!
Keep a record of what happened – photographs of your involvement, of the posters, the presentations, people's comments – has the event changed their minds? Record/video them?

October 28
Start marketing event – posters, school newsletter, school website?
Keep copies of the evidence.

Take action

When you have decided on your action, get together with the rest of the team and work out how you are going to go about planning and putting your idea into practice.

Checkpoints

Things to record and remember:

- how you decided on your action. Was it democratic?
- why the issue is important
- the links to Citizenship.

Getting you thinking

Team people

It is tempting to have a team made up of your friends, but they are often just like you. That's why you are friends! A good team has people with a mix of skills. Just look at the things that must be done and you will see that you need a range of people. Depending on the size of your group, you may need to double up the tasks. A good team adds up to more than each of the members individually.

Someone who is good at leading ideas

Someone who is good at leading research

Someone who is good at leading communication

Someone who will get things done

Someone who will lead the group

Working in a team

If you are working in a team, you are **collaborating**. This sounds easy, but people don't always agree, so it is important to think about the way your team works before you begin. You need to think about what you will do if people fall out! People get fed up if someone refuses to agree with everyone else. People get fed up if someone isn't pulling their weight. How will you resolve situations like this? It's important to know the answers to these questions before you begin – and set the ground rules.

Good teamwork

Be enthusiastic.

Have clear objectives.

Have a logical plan.

Have a good mix of relevant skills.

Learn from setbacks.

Teamwork

Everyone takes responsibility.

Everyone understands their roles and tasks.

Work in an informal environment – humour helps.

Group members listen and accept constructive feedback.

Everyone listens and gives constructive feedback.

Brainstorming

If you are to create an environment in which everyone is free to express their point of view, brainstorming is a good way to open the discussion. Use a large piece of paper and put everyone's ideas down. Everyone's ideas are valuable – so no one should be ridiculed. You can then work out which ideas are really useful.

Making decisions

Before you begin, you need to decide how you will go about making decisions. People do not agree all the time, but if you are to move forward, you must all agree – or agree to disagree. You've learned much about democracy, so this is the time to apply it. Take a vote!

A vote can help to overcome all sorts of problems when people want to do different things. This may happen at any stage in the process. Remember to use your research in making your decisions. Sometimes people will take a point of view without really thinking it through. Pages 166–7 on research will help you to weigh up your research and decide on its value.

In the exam, you might be asked about how you made decisions, so note down each time you do so – and the outcome.

Remember to be realistic!

It is easy to get carried away! It is easy for your enthusiasm to lead you to take on more than you can manage. Time and resources are limited – so be sensible. Listen to a team member who is cautious and questions whether you can achieve the big ideas that are on the table. Being unable to complete your action will make it more difficult to answer the question in the exam.

Take action

Identify your group. Everyone should set out their strengths and weaknesses relevant to the roles you need in the group. Use this to work out who is assigned to do what. Talk about the way you will work together and what it means to collaborate. Set the ground rules for your discussions and planning.

Checkpoints

Once you have set up you team and worked out how you will collaborate, check that your teacher is happy with what you have done.

While you are planning and carrying out your action, keep a note of how the team has worked. You will need it for revision.

Key terms
collaborating: working together towards an outcome

Getting you thinking

1 Why might you want to find out what people think?

2 Why do you need to be careful when planning the questions?

3 Why do you need to be careful when asking the questions?

4 How do you decide who to ask?

When planning your action, one thing you need to think about is what you need to know. You may not have a clear idea of people's views. Once you have found out what people think, you may be able to structure your action more effectively.

You may think you know about people's opinions, but it is easy to be misled. It is a good idea to test your views so you can take everything into account when you make your plans.

Drawing up a questionnaire

- Before you begin – make sure you know exactly what you want to find out.

- Make the questions very clear – especially if people will fill in the questionnaire on their own.

- Make the questions quick – people won't spend long on the questionnaire.

- Avoid leading questions (they often start with 'Don't you think that … ?') – they give you the answer you want to hear but it may not be what people really think.

- Is the order of the questions important? If so, work out which should come first, second, third …

- Do you need to know:

  – how old people are?

  – what gender they are?

  – how much they earn?

  – whether they are healthy?

- These are sensitive questions, so ask them carefully. Do you want short, sharp answers? If so, use **closed questions** – they often have yes/no/don't know answers.

- Do you want more thoughtful answers? If so, use **open questions** – you will find out about people's opinions and why they hold them.
- Avoid obvious questions – no one will answer 'Yes' to 'Would you be cruel to animals?'

Work out the results

When you have used your questionnaire to carry out a survey, you need to work out what the answers mean.

The results of closed questions are easy to understand. You simply have to add up the number of each different response. Draw up a tally sheet showing the possible answers for each question. Count up how many people gave each answer and put the number in the box. This will give you quantitative data.

Question 1: How often do you go swimming?

Once a week or more	Once every two weeks	Once a month	Less often
ⲎⲎ I	III	ⲎⲎ	II

The line drawn across four tally marks makes it five. This makes counting easy.

Open questions ask people for their opinions and ideas. Read them carefully in order to decide how to divide them up. Many people come up with fairly standard views, so you can put them into separate groups. Work out how many you have in each group and note any ideas that stand out from the others. Jot down some good examples of what people were thinking. These will help your report. Sometimes people offer very strange ideas. These can also be noted in order to show the range of answers.

Open questions give you qualitative data.

Displaying your results

Very often you want other people to know your findings, so you need to make them as clear as possible. Graphs and charts will help you to do this. Bar charts and pie charts are good ways of showing data.

If you put the results into a spreadsheet, you can choose a wide variety of different sorts of graph to show your evidence. Be careful to choose the one that suits your data.

Take action

Do you need to find out what people think? If so, set about writing a questionnaire. Think carefully about the guidelines provided here. You might start with closed questions and have an open question or two at the end. Make sure you are not asking leading questions. This can be quite hard when you really believe in something.

Checkpoints

Try out your questionnaire on someone like the people you are planning to ask. If some questions don't work, change them. Using the wrong questions is a waste of time!

Key terms
closed questions: ask for short factual answers
open questions: ask people to express a point of view or give a longer answer

Getting you thinking

Who can you persuade?

Students from Deptford Green School were fed up because of the mess made by pigeons nesting under a bridge which they walked under on the way to school. They organised a visit to Metronet, the organisation responsible for the bridge. It was agreed that work would be carried out on the bridge during the summer holidays to prevent the pigeons roosting. Result!

1 Why do you think the students picked this issue?

2 How did they set about solving the problem?

3 Why do you think Metronet agreed to carry out the work?

The role of advocacy

Pressure groups and other organisations want to persuade people to change what they do or the way they do things. If you look at the websites of charities and pressure groups, you will find they are campaigning about issues that matter to them. This is known as advocacy, which you found out about in Theme D, 'Power and influence'. If your action involves persuasion, you will need to work out the best way to go about it. Young people are often very good at this. When they believe in a cause or an issue, they argue and defend it until they have convinced the listener! You just have to put these skills into a Citizenship context.

How to be an advocate

Before you start, you need to work out the answers to some questions.

- **What do we want?** You must have a clear vision that you can put into words and will be clear and logical for other people.

- **Who can make it happen?** You must identify the people you need to persuade.

- **What do they think at the moment?** Find out whether they are likely to agree with you.

- **What do they need to hear?** Depending on the answer to the last question, you will need to work out the line to take with them. Be prepared to answer their questions.

Once you have worked out the answers to these questions, you can make a plan.

Dealing with different points of view?

Once you try to persuade people about your issue, you will realise that people have different points of view. You need to manage their views if you want to achieve success.

Try to put yourself into the other person's shoes. What do they have to consider before coming to a decision? If your issue involves spending money, they may have to work out where the money comes from and if it is more important to spend it on your cause.

Remember this when putting your case together. It would be good to make some sensible suggestions about how to solve the problems that may arise.

Building your case

A statement: state your objective clearly and briefly.

↓

Evidence: your secondary research must be good. Do you have primary research to support your case?

↓

Example: people always like real examples of the outcome. What effect would your action have?

↓

Goal: link your objective to the example.

↓

What do you want other people to do?
Sum up clearly.

Things to remember

People are busy, so don't take too long to get your message over.

Leave your audience with some material about your cause – and what you want – so they can refer to it later. Send them a summary of the meeting. This is useful if they have agreed to act. They may need reminding!

If there is some acceptance of your plans but also some resistance, you may need to come back to **negotiate**. Work out where you might compromise on your plans.

How to get the message across

It is important to choose the right way to inform people about your cause. People respond in different ways to the way a message is given. Think carefully about the best way to get the message across to your audience.

 In person – lobbying visits, community meetings, protests, demonstrations

 In print – newspapers, magazines, newsletters, posters, leaflets, pamphlets, letters to decision makers

 Electronically – radio, television, video and film

 Internet – blogs, social media websites, YouTube, mobile technology

 Drama and music – theatre, songs, music, poems, dance

Take action

Once you have decided on your action, you will need to decide who to talk to.

Think of people who are easy to get hold of. If you are concerned that some countries still use child labour, don't attempt to talk to the country's president! You might try to get a view from Oxfam or a business that has been accused of using child labour.

Checkpoints

If you want to talk to the head teacher, make an appointment. If there are several of you who want to talk about the same thing, work together because everyone is very busy.

If you want to talk to the council, try the local councillor first. They will tell you where to go next if they can't deal with it themselves.

If you need to talk to other organisations, email works well because it is quick. Make sure you keep your email and the replies for your records.

Key terms

negotiate: the process of discussing something with someone in order to reach an agreement

Getting you thinking

1 How can the local radio station help with your campaign?

2 What other media might you use?

3 What would you need to think about before talking to the media?

How to spread your message

What's your message?

What is the single most important point that you want your target audience to remember?

This is your 'message'.

Your message should now be the focus for every conversation that your pressure group has with the public.

What's the evidence?

What facts support your argument?

You must give the target audience a reason to believe you.

Who is your target audience?

A target audience is the group of people you are trying to reach with your message. Who is most interested in your point of view? Why?

For example, if an issue will have an impact on the environment, you might choose young parents as a target audience. They may be concerned about how the issue affects their children's future.

Presenting your message

Present your message in an interesting and emotive way. What headline could you use to grab the attention of the reader?

What sort of words could you use to stir their emotions? 'Destroy', 'hopeless', 'saved', 'heroic' or 'desolate'? These words are often used for the impact they have on a reader.

How to persuade people

Put across your point of view

Ask questions and use the answers as a starting point. You may even provide the answers yourself – it will start them thinking. This gets people interested in what you have to say, and helps them to agree with your point.

Try:

- Why should we be interested?
- Haven't we heard enough?
- Why do they oppose/propose this?
- What will we gain from this?

Make it easy for people to agree with you

If you want people to agree with your point of view, show them that you have lots in common. If you like the same things, you are more likely to get on!

You need to do this before starting to talk about the topic you want to discuss.

Try:

- As a member of this community for many years …
- We all want the best solution …

Think about the opposition

Consider the opposition's point of view before you start. You'll be able to answer their questions if you are prepared. This shows everyone that you have a balanced point of view.

Always have a short, snappy ending

End your argument on a high note using a short, snappy sentence, such as 'We need a school crossing NOW!'

How to approach the local media

The local media is very important to the success of a local campaign because:

- it affects the local community
- it's a great way of getting free publicity and attracting support from other people.

Preparing a press release

A press release should tell the journalists who work at the local paper, radio or TV station all they need to know about your campaign:

- what the issue is
- why it is of interest to the local community
- contact details for you and your group
- suggestions of interesting pictures for newspaper and television.

It should be written in snappy language, like a newspaper article, and be aimed at your target audience. Press releases are sometimes printed in a newspaper with very little editing, so try to use a catchy headline.

When your press release is ready, find out the name and address, telephone number or email of local newspapers, radio and television stations.

Write a letter or send an email to the contact name that you have been given. The letter should explain why you feel so strongly about the issue and ask the journalist to contact you for any further information.

Take action

Work out:

- What's your message?
- Who is your target audience?
- Why will your message appeal to your target audience?
- How will you sell it to them?
- Who do you need to talk to in your local area? Remember that they are probably people of power and influence – so their evidence will be helpful.

Checkpoints

Discuss making contact with the local media with your teacher first.

Ask for a copy of any interviews. It will all add to your evidence.

Getting you thinking

SAVE LIVES – STOP KNIVES!

More than 1000 people joined the families and friends of knife and gun crime victims in a protest march across London.

The idea for the People's March was started on Facebook by Sharon Singh and Gemma Olway from South West London. It received the backing of several national newspapers, which promoted it to the public.

The marchers chanted 'Stop the knives, save lives' as they walked through London. Onlookers clapped and some motorists beeped their horns in a show of support.

The minister responsible for the police spoke to the crowd, saying: 'If your local community isn't doing enough, speak to your local councillor and if they don't do enough, sack them at the next election or get hold of your MP and if they don't do anything, sack them.'

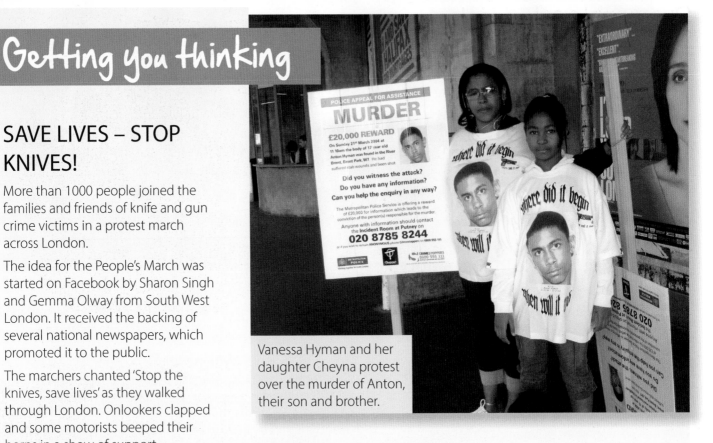

Vanessa Hyman and her daughter Cheyna protest over the murder of Anton, their son and brother.

1 Why do you think Sharon and Gemma decided to organise a protest march?

2 What effect do you think the backing of national newspapers offered?

3 What reception did the marchers get from passersby?

4 Why do you think the minister responsible for the police spoke to the crowd?

5 What advice did he give them? Why do you think he said this?

Why protest?

Protest and marches are very powerful because they attract the attention of the public and offer them the opportunity to join in or show their support in other ways. They are often used:

- when controversial decisions are being made
- to draw attention to an issue
- to commemorate an anniversary.

A march or protest should not be organised lightly. If badly planned, a protest can be a flop, upset the general public and even break the law. Making life difficult for ordinary people should be avoided. Truck drivers blocked motorways and city centres because the price of diesel was too high. Even though many people supported their cause, the resulting traffic jams upset just as many.

Whether to protest

It is only worth organising a march or a protest if:

- public opinion is so strong that a fairly good turnout can be guaranteed
- it can be planned sufficiently far in advance to meet the legal requirements
- it can be well publicised and promoted
- it can be well managed on the day.

If a full-scale march or protest is too large a project, smaller events might be easier to organise. A demonstration before a council meeting or at a shop that is ignoring employment law are much simpler to organise and can have a direct effect.

Questions to ask

Any event needs to be targeted carefully and set up to have maximum effect, so there are some questions that must be asked before you begin.

- Who are you trying to reach?
- What are you trying to achieve?
- What needs to be done and who will do it?
- Are there any costs? How will they be paid?
- Whatever the event, the police should be informed – and you must check with the school that they are happy for you to go ahead.
- Have you checked the health and safety regulations?
- Is there likely to be opposition? If so, work out how you will deal with it.
- Can we get the media interested? The whole point of a protest is to be noticed!

Publicising the event

The grand finale

The event mustn't just fizzle out at the end. The knife crime march ended in Hyde Park. The crowd was addressed by the Metropolitan Police Commissioner, a government minister and a video message from the Prime Minister. Not many events can attract such high status people, but finding a high-profile person who believes in your issue will help to get the message across.

A protest can have a big impact – particularly when it has media coverage.

Take action

Plan the action carefully. Ask yourself:

- What are you trying to achieve?
- Who is going to do what?
- Who do you need to contact?
- Who is on your side? Will they help?
- How will you work out whether it has been a success?

Checkpoints

Before you think about planning an event outside school, check with your teacher.

Getting you thinking

Save my school!

Aimee said: 'I was racing to save my school.

It's such a good school – it is really unfair to close it down.

I tried to use the success of the triathlon to highlight what I see as a failure of the council in their decision to shut the school.'

1 How is Aimee showing her Citizenship skills?

2 Why does she want to make a difference?

3 Why did she pick this strategy?

4 What do you think she had to do to plan this activity?

5 What sort of evidence do you think she collected?

6 How does this activity relate to the content of the course?

How you aimed to meet your objectives

Aimee really didn't want her school to close. She worked out how she could communicate the issue to as many people as possible. As a triathlete, she knew that the press would cover her next race – and she was right, as the picture above shows.

In your action plan you set out how you planned to meet your objectives. What strategies did you use?

Did you:

- produce leaflets, posters, banners or placards?
- run an assembly?
- put on a play?
- set up a website?
- hold a meeting?
- send letters or emails?
- talk to local radio or newspapers?
- hold a protest?
- lobby your councillors, MP or MEP?
- use any other strategy?

Whichever strategies you used, you need to know why you selected them and how you participated.

How did you communicate with others?

Who were you trying to persuade:

- the general public?
- people in positions of power?
- other school students?
- parents?

What strategies did you use for each group?

When you set about persuading people, you need to be able to present a good argument. There are moments when making a lot of noise can be useful. If you want to raise the issue with a lot of people, a demonstration might work well. If you want to persuade people in power, you need to have very good arguments on your side. If you are going to persuade them, you also need to know their point of view. It is much easier to fight if you know how the opposition thinks.

Think about how your participation meets these needs.

Gather evidence of your action and how you made a contribution

You will need to collect evidence of your action, so you can revise for the exam. Make it fun, so you will remember it!

- Photos are great because many people have a visual memory. Placards and banners are too big, but you can take pictures of them being used as evidence of how you communicated.

- A video can show the work involved in your campaign. An audio recording of a meeting or a presentation about carrying out your activity gives a clear picture of how you were working.

- A PowerPoint presentation that explains or persuades people of your point of view will help you to remember.

- A website that lets people know your plans or persuades them to support you is helpful evidence as it shows just what you were trying to do and how you went about it.

- If you investigate what people think, you may use a questionnaire. This, together with the results, shows the way you worked and what you found out.

- You might write letters or emails to explain, persuade or justify your point of view. These are useful because they will remind you of your findings.

Gathering all the information as you go along will help you to put it all together. It's very easy to forget exactly what happened and when!

Take action

Work out how you are going to campaign and how you are hoping to change people's thinking.

Work out how you are going to gather the evidence. Make sure you keep it safe so you can revise for the exam.

Checkpoints

Get organised! Your record is important, so build it into every part of your action.

For example, a letter or email to an important person would show your arguments. A questionnaire would help you to find out what people think – and how best to persuade them. It is also important that you show how the evidence you have gathered can be used to support arguments and make judgements.

What views did others hold?

You need to remember what other people thought but, rather than writing about it, you can use other forms of evidence.

- The local media can be a useful source of other people's points of view. If you are campaigning about something local, you can be sure that they will be involved. Look out for press cuttings.

- Has the opposition got a website?

- You could interview people and record the conversation.

When Oxford University built a new centre for medical research, animal rights protestors tried to prevent it happening. Supporters of the development took to the streets as well.

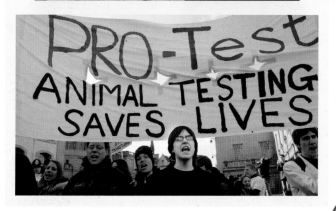

Getting you thinking

Did your action achieve its goals?

A Citizenship action always aims to make a difference. At the beginning, you set your objectives. It's now time to work out just how successful you were.

- If you ran a Fair Trade day, did you influence other students' views? Was there a demand to sell Fair Trade products in school? If your fellow students are now persuading their families to buy Fair Trade products, you are having an effect because people growing cocoa beans or coffee or making clothes will have a better standard of living.

- If your group was trying to persuade the local council to provide more sports facilities or to light a subway to make it safer, what was the result? Don't worry if the council didn't accept your idea immediately. If you have got a councillor to support your idea, you have made a difference. They will probably bring it up again in the next financial year. Ask them to do so. These things can take time!

Very often the outcome is a compromise.

- A new supermarket might want to cut down trees to build an access road. Perhaps they changed the line of the road and saved some of the trees.

- The council wants to close the skate park. Perhaps it might just be opened at the weekend instead.

Did you choose the right strategy?

When you made your plan, you will have put together a series of activities to achieve your objectives. What activities did you select and why? Did they work? How did you come to the conclusion that it wasn't working? If not, can you explain why? What did you do instead?

When looking back on your action, might you have chosen a completely different path to achieve you objective?

If you changed your objectives during the campaign, explain how and why. Did it make your objectives more achievable?

You will work out whether your action was successful and how it affected your learning.

5.11 The impact of your action

What did you learn?

Carrying out a Citizenship action involves lots of learning. You will have learned about the skills you need to research, influence, persuade, communicate, negotiate and work as a team. There's lots of learning in planning and carrying out your action too. You have had to work out how to make decisions and judge whether things are working. If not, you'll have had to decide to change the plans.

You will also have been putting your Citizenship knowledge into practice. Your action will have helped you to understand ideas of democracy as well as ideas that underpin your action.

Has your action changed your views?

I'm even more committed!

When you came up with the idea for your issue, you probably thought it was worthwhile. You will have done both secondary and primary research. You will have listened to people's point of view. Your work may have increased your conviction that things need to be done.

I've changed my mind!

Citizenship is all about points of view.

If you wanted the council to enclose a basketball court or set up a skate park, you might have listened to the arguments about how the council spends its money. Perhaps other people have pointed out that spending money to meet your plans would mean spending less on old people or reducing the hours the library is open.

Did you decide which was more important?

Checkpoints

Having completed your action and worked out how and why it was effective, you will need to make sure that your records are in order. In the exam you will be asked to make a short statement about what you did, so the examiner can see if your answers make sense. There will be some practical questions about the skills and knowledge you used, and a more open-ended question for which you have to build an argument.

Your teacher will provide you with materials to help you keep your records throughout the action. Don't lose them – you will need them!

5.12 Bringing it all together

As part of your course, you have been a member of a group that organised and took part in a Citizenship action. In no more than 20 words, write the title of your Citizenship action.

After a student was hurt in an accident outside school, we decided to campaign for a 20 mph speed limit.

This uses the 20 words to give the examiner a clear idea of your action.

1. When working in a group, collaboration is important. Explain two ways in which your team collaborated.

   1. We collaborated by doing all the planning together. We all sat down in a meeting to make a step-by-step plan of what we were going to do.

   2. We also collaborated by dividing up the roles and things that needed to be done so we could be more efficient. Amanda and I wrote the questionnaire for school while Ahmed and Phoebe did the one for the neighbours.
   (2 marks)

   The student shows that they understand what collaboration means and gives two clear points with strong links to their action.

2. People involved in taking Citizenship action in their community choose from a range of methods to find out about people's views.

   Explain one method you chose. *(2 marks)*

   We used questionnaires because we needed to find out whether people agreed with us and whether people had different points of view. It meant that we could check what different groups of people thought too.

   Explain whether the method was successful. *(2 marks)*

   The questionnaires we gave out in school were very successful because we got nearly all of them back so we knew what people thought. The ones we gave to the neighbours were less successful because not all of them were returned.

   There are two marks for each section of this question, so it important to make two points. The student does this very well and earns all four marks.

3. Citizenship actions aim to bring about change. Explain two ways in which you planned to bring about change through your action. *(4 marks)*

   Method 1: We talked to our local councillor because she represents democracy in our area. We also knew that she would give us advice on what we needed to do to make change happen.

Method 2: We also met the council officers who are the experts on transport in the local area. We needed to persuade them of our case if the council was to agree to change the speed limit.

> The student has given two clear processes they carried out in trying to achieve change, and explained why they did each of them. Note the use of a Citizenship concept in the answer. This shows the examiner that you have a good grasp of its meaning and how to use it.

Extended writing

'Good communication is the most important requirement for an effective Citizenship action.' How far do you agree with this view?
You **must** base your answer on your experience of your own Citizenship action.
Give reasons for your opinion, showing that you have considered another point of view. *(12 marks)*

Our campaign was trying to persuade the local council to put a 20 mph speed limit on the road outside school. Communication was very important to us because we had to talk to the right people and get support from people in school, their families and residents in our neighbourhood.

> The question says: 'You must base your answer on your experience of your own Citizenship action'. Here, and all the way through, the student bases their answer on how they carried out their action.

We had to work out how best to communicate with each group. This means that communication is important but it has to be chosen carefully to be effective. We told people in school about it when we sent out a questionnaire asking if people agreed with us. They nearly all did. We sent a similar questionnaire to houses near the school. Their answers were more mixed because some didn't want to go at 20 when school was closed. We didn't get answers from everyone – which meant that our evidence wasn't so strong. If we had spoken to them all, it might have been better but there wasn't time.

> The student shows here that they understand the strengths and weaknesses of different sorts of communication and is evaluating their activities.

At first we emailed the local councillor to ask what she thought. She replied that she agreed but we needed some more information about how to go about contacting the council as a whole, so we asked her to a meeting. Sometimes it is best to talk face to face. She told us that we needed to contact the transport department. The people there would need evidence, so we put together a document with all the information we had collected to set out our case and try to persuade them. As our research showed that other schools in the area had 20 mph limits, we thought our case was strong.

> You need to show that you can build a good argument. This paragraph shows that the student understands how and why different sorts of communication are important.

All the way through, we also had to communicate with each other. We chose our methods of communication carefully — but if we hadn't, it would have been a waste of time. All sorts of things can go wrong if members of the team don't tell each other what they are doing or what they have found out when doing research. We had regular meetings to share things and also sent emails round, with everyone copied in.

> Here, the student develops their understanding of communication by showing that it is important within the team as well as with the audience they want to talk to.

Communication is very important but it is not the only skill that makes Citizenship action work. Without planning, our action probably would not have worked as it would have been a mess. We also had to work together as a team to make the most of our strengths and get things done. The research we carried out was also important because we needed it to build our case for a 20 mph limit. Negotiation was very important when talking to councillors and the officers at the council because we had to be prepared to argue our case.

> You are asked to show that you understand concepts, terms and issues. This paragraph shows that the student understands the range of skills required for a Citizenship action.

Without these skills, we would not have had much to communicate as we would not have worked out who to talk to and how to go about it and we would not have built a very good case.

Communication is very important but, as I have shown, without the other skills, it is not much use.

> The student has clearly argued both sides of the case but the other point of view is not so strong. There is evidence, but it could have been in greater depth.

Glossary

ACAS: an organisation that tries to resolve disputes between employers and employees

accountable: if you are accountable for something, you are responsible for it and have to explain your actions

Act: a law passed by Parliament

Act of Parliament: a law passed by Parliament

advocacy: publicly supporting an issue or proposal

arrested: a person who is arrested is held against their will because they are suspected of committing a crime

Assembly: a body of people elected to decide on some areas of spending in a region

asylum seeker: someone who says he or she is a refugee, but whose claim has not yet been definitively evaluated

back benchers: MPs who do not hold office in the government or opposition; they sit on the back benches in the House of Commons

barrister: a lawyer who represents and speaks for their clients in court

bi-cameral: the UK Parliament is bi-cameral because it has two Houses, the House of commons and the House of Lords

biased: in favour one thing over another, unfairly

bill: a proposal to change something into law

Black Rod: the person who has ceremonial duties in the Palace of Westminster, including bringing MPs to the House of Lords for the State Opening of Parliament

boycott: to refuse to use or have anything to do with something

British constitution: the laws and conventions which set down how the UK is governed

Budget: the process each year when the Chancellor of the Exchequer explains how the government will raise and spend its money

business rates: a form of tax paid by all the businesses in an area. The amount a business pays depends on the rent that could be charged for its premises

Cabinet: a group of MPs who head major government departments. It meets weekly to make decisions about how government policy will be carried out. Senior Ministers from the Lords are also represented

cabinet: the main decision-making body of the council

canvassing: when people try to persuade others to vote for their party in an election

case law or precedent: once a decision has been made in a court it becomes law in all future cases containing the same material facts and it must be followed by all lower courts

censorship: limiting the information given to the general public by the government

census: an official count of the population to find out about the changes taking place

Chancellor of the Exchequer: the member of the government who is responsible for the country's finances

charity: an organisation set up to provide help and raise money for those in need

Chief Executive: an employee of the council, responsible for the smooth running of services

Citizens Advice Bureau (CAB): an organisation that offers free advice on consumer and other legal matters

civil law: this covers disputes between individuals or groups. Civil law cases are often about rights

closed questions: ask for short factual answers

closed-list system: a form of PR in which a party puts forward a list of candidates in the order they will be elected

coalition: a government made of more than one party. It is formed when no one party has enough seats to form a government

collaborating: working together towards an outcome

collective bargaining: negotiating the terms of employment between an employer and a group of workers

Commonwealth: a voluntary group of independent countries, some of which were former British colonies

Commonwealth of Nations: a voluntary group of independent countries

community: a group of people who are in close contact and who share common interests and values

community cohesion: creating a community where there is a sense of belonging for all communities and people's different backgrounds are valued

community sentence: a sentence which allows people to continue to live in the community under certain conditions

compensation: making amends for something; something given to make good a loss

constituency: the area represented by an MP

consumer: a person who buys goods or services for their own use

contract of employment: a document that details an employee's and employer's responsibilities for a particular job

convention: an agreement (often between governments)

council: a group of people who are elected to look after the affairs of a town, district or county

council tax: a tax paid by everyone who lives in an area. It is based on the value of their house

councillor: a member of a local council, elected by people in the area

county court: a local court that has limited powers in civil cases

criminal law: this deals with offences such as murder and drug dealing. These cases are between the Crown Prosecution Service (acting for all citizens) and the offender

crown court: courts held in towns in England and Wales where judges hear criminal cases

customs duty: taxes on products bought from other countries

declaration: a document setting down aims and intentions

democracy: government by the people, either directly or through elected representatives

devolution: the transfer of power from central to regional government

dictator: a national leader who makes all the decisions for the country, without reference to the population

digital democracy: the use of online methods to support election campaigns and voting

direct action: action to bring about change, such as demonstrations or strikes

direct democracy: a form of democracy in which everyone votes on every decision in a referendum

discharge: not being sentenced for a minor crime; it can be conditional

discrimination: treating someone less favourably because of their colour, ethnic origins, gender or disability

dismissal: when an employer ends an employee's contract of employment

diversity: the range of different groups that make up a wider population

economic migrant: a person who travels from one country or area to another in order to improve their standard of living

economy: this is made up of all the organisations that provide goods and services, and all the individuals and organisations that buy them

editor: the person who is responsible for the content of a newspaper, television or radio programme

Editors' Code of Practice: guidelines for the media and journalists about the information they gather and how they obtain and use it

election: selection of one or more people for an official position by voting

emigration: leaving your homeland to live in another country

employment tribunal: a type of court dealing only with disagreements over employment laws

entrepreneur: a person who sets up a business and takes on financial risks in the hope of making a profit

European Union: a group of 28 countries which work together in fields such as the environment, social issues, the economy and trade

Fair Trade: a system of buying and selling products that aims to pay the producer a fair price

first past the post: an electoral system where voters have one vote in their constituency and the candidate with the most votes wins

free trade: trade between countries which is not restricted by things like high taxes on imports

front benchers: MPs who hold office in the government or opposition. They sit on the front benches in the House of Commons

general election: an election for a new government. In the UK, these take place at least every five years

Geneva Convention: an internationally accepted set of rules on the treatment of people in war

genocide: mass murder of a racial, national or religious group

government revenue: the money raised by the government

Green Paper: this puts forward ideas that the government wants discussed before it starts to develop a policy

harassment: repeatedly threatening, humiliating or pestering someone

High Court: the court where judges hear cases on serious crimes

homophobic: fearing or hating gay or bisexual people

House of Commons: the more powerful of the two parts of the British Parliament. Its members are elected by the public

human rights: things that people are morally or legally allowed to do or have

hustings: a meeting at which candidates in an election speak to the voters

identity: who or what someone or something is

identity card: a card that establishes someone's identity

immigration: coming to another country to live there

inclusive education: schooling that involves everyone, regardless of disability or non disability

indirect action: making your case by persuasion rather than action

integration: bringing different groups of people together in society

interest group or pressure group: a group of people that tries to change public opinion or government policy to its own views or beliefs

investigative journalism: the deep investigation of a topic of interest, such as serious crimes, political corruption or corporate wrongdoing

journalist: a person who gathers news and produces reports for the media

judge: a person who decides questions of law in a court

judicial review: a review carried out by the High Court to decide whether a decision made by a public body has been made properly

jury: a group of people who decide if someone is guilty in a court of law

legal right: a right that is protected by law

libel: writing incorrect things about people

lobbying: trying to persuade a politician or the government to change the law or take a particular action

magistrates' court: a court held before two or more public officers dealing with minor crimes

Magna Carta: a charter of rights which the English barons forced King John to sign in 1215

majority: the party with a majority has won a bigger proportion of the votes than the others

manifesto: a published statement of the aims and policies of a political party

mayor: a member of the council who is selected to be its representative on ceremonial occasions; in some areas they are also the elected leader

media: ways of communicating with large numbers of people

mediator: acting as a go-between between people in dispute in order to resolve the problem

Member of Parliament: a person who has been elected to represent a part of the country in Parliament

Member of the European Parliament: a person who has been elected to represent a part of the country in the European Parliament

member state: a country that is a member of the EU

MEP: Member of the European Parliament

micro-credit: making small loans to individuals to help them help themselves

Minister of State: an assistant to the Secretary of State

minority: a small part of a larger group of people

mitigating factors: reasons why an offender might be given a lighter sentence

moral right: the responsibility of people to behave in a moral way towards others

multiple identity: when a person feels they have more than one identity

National Living Wage: the minimum amount to be paid to an employee over the age of 25

National Minimum Wage: the minimum amount to be paid to an employee

NATO: the North Atlantic Treaty Organisation, whose members work together to defend each other

negotiate: the process of discussing something with someone in order to reach an agreement

Neighbourhood Watch: a scheme in which members of the community take responsibility for keeping an eye on each other's property to prevent crime

neighbourhood: a local area within which people live as neighbours, sharing living space and interests

non-governmental organisations: organisations, not run by government, that support people in need of help

Office for National Statistics: the organisation that collects data about what is happening in the UK

Office of Fair Trading: a government office that can take action against traders who break the law

ombudsman: an official who is appointed to investigate individuals' complaints against a company or an organisation

open questions: ask people to express a point of view or give a longer answer

opposition: political parties that are not in power

Parliamentary inquiry: an enquiry set up to investigate actions taken by government departments and public bodies

Parliamentary sovereignty: Parliament is the top legal body and can pass new laws or stop old laws

political party: an organised group of people with common aims who put up candidates for elections

political rights: rights to take part in elections and other democratic activities

polling station: a place where votes are cast; often a school, library or village hall

press freedom: the ability of the press to give information and express opinion

primary research: new research to answer a particular question

Prime Minister: the leader of the majority party in the House of Commons and the leader of the government

probation officer: someone who writes court reports on offenders and supervises them in the community

propaganda: information, which might be biased or misleading, used to promote a political cause or point of view

proportional representation: an electoral system in which the number of seats a party wins is roughly proportional to its share of the votes in an election

public institutions: organisations provided by the government, like schools and hospitals

public opinion: views held by the general public on a particular issue

public services: services provided by the state, like policing, education and refuse collection

qualitative data: deals with descriptions and cannot be counted

quantitative data: deals with information that can be counted or measured

racism: the idea that some people of different origins are not as good as others

recorder: a barrister or solicitor of at least 10 years' experience, who acts as a part-time judge in a crown court

redundancy: when a person loses their job because the job doesn't need to be done any more

referendum: a vote by the whole electorate on a particular issue

refugee: a person who has been forced to leave their country in order to escape war, persecution, or natural disaster

rehabilitation programmes: programmes which help people to overcome problems so they can avoid committing crimes in future

reoffend: to commit a crime more than once

representative democracy: a form of democracy in which people elect a representative to make decisions for them

respect: show consideration for someone's feelings, wishes or rights

responsibility: something it is your duty to do or to look after

restorative justice: a system of criminal justice which aims to rehabilitate offenders through meeting and talking to victims and the community

rule of law: a country is governed by law and all residents must obey the law – so no one is above the law

sanction: a penalty for breaking rules, especially in international situations

scrutiny: to examine something carefully

secondary research: published research collected by other people

Secretary of State: an MP who is in charge of a government department such as health or defence

select committee: one of the committees that check and report on the work of government departments

Shadow Cabinet: MPs from the main opposition party who 'shadow' MPs who head major government departments

slander: saying incorrect things about people

small claims court: a local court, which hears civil cases involving small amounts of money

solicitor: a lawyer who gives legal advice and may speak for their clients in court

Speaker: the MP elected to act as chairman for debates in the House of Commons

special constable: a volunteer police officer

spin-doctor: someone who tries to get certain stories into the public eye and to make bad news sound better

staff associations: associations of employees with some of the functions of a trade union, such as representing their members in discussions with management

sue: to make a claim against someone or something

tariffs: taxes to be paid on a some imports or exports

the executive: makes policy and puts it into practice. It is made up of the Prime Minister, Cabinet and Civil Service

the judiciary: makes judgments about the law. It is made up of judges and magistrates in courts

the legislature: makes laws. It is made up of the House of Lords and House of Commons

tolerant: open-minded, accepting

trade unions: organisations that look after the interests of a group of employees

Trading Standards Department: an official body that enforces consumer-based law

tribunals: these are set up to resolve certain types of dispute, such as employment issues

turnout: the percentage of people who vote in an election

United Nations: an international organisation that tries to encourage peace, cooperation and friendship between countries

victimisation: discriminating against someone unfairly

voluntary organisations: bodies whose activities are carried out for reasons other than profit, but which do not include any public or local authority funding

volunteer: someone who works for free for a community

vote: to choose a candidate in an election

ward: an area that forms a separate part of a local council

White Paper: this puts government policy up for discussion before it becomes law

young offenders: offenders between the ages of 10 and 17

youth court: a court that deals with young offenders

youth justice system: the part of the justice system that deals with young people

Index

ACKNOWLEDGEMENTS

The Publishers gratefully acknowledge the following for permission to reproduce copyright material. While every effort has been made to trace copyright holders, if any have been inadvertently overlooked, the Publishers will be pleased to make the necessary arrangements at the first opportunity.

Text extract acknowledgements:
Tables and charts on pages 10, 11, 12, 14, 127, Immigration and Emigration; Ethnic groups 2001 and 2011, England and Wales; Changes in religious beliefs in the UK; UK Population 1964–2014; and Adult participation in selected leisure activities, Source: *Social Trends*, adapted from data from the Office for National Statistics; Map on page 11, Ethnic minorities by region, Source: *2011 Census*, Office for National Statistics adapted from data from the Office for National Statistics; and Figures on page 14, 72, United Kingdom Population, 2014 and Total Managed expenditure and Total revenue, Source: HM Treasury, adapted from data from the Office for National Statistics licensed under the Open Government Licence v.3.0; An extract on page 21 from 'Dignity and Respect Community Principles', https://www.essex.ac.uk/dignity/community_principles.aspx, copyright © 2016 University of Essex. All rights reserved; Extract on page 23 adapted from "Education is the answer" by Alex Ferguson, *Kick it Out Magazine*, October 2001, copyright © Kick It Out; Extract on page 26 from 'Supporting new communities' adapted from the Fenland District Council Community Cohesion document, copyright © 2016 Fenland District Council; Extract on page 26 adapted from 'Supporting new communities' adapted from https://oycevents.wordpress.com/about/, copyright © Oldham Youth Council, 2016; Extract on page 27 from 'International Week' adapted from http://www.berger.hackney.sch.uk/2015/international-week. Reproduced with permission of Berger Primary School; Figure on page 40, 'Firework injuries in the UK'. Source: Firework injury statistics, 2005 BERR. Contains public sector information licensed under the Open Government Licence v.3.0; Extract on page 51 about the Human Rights Act adapted from 'Save Our Human Rights Act' https://www.liberty-human-rights.org.uk/campaigning/save-our-human-rights-act-0. Reproduced with permission of Liberty; Extract on page 51 about the Human Rights Act from *Conservative Manifesto 2015*. Source: The Conservative Party; Quotations on pages 56 and 62 from Scott Mann, MP. Reproduced with kind permission; Extract on page 68 adapted from "Scottish independence - the YES comment: A fairer Scotland is within our grasp" by Blair Jenkins, *The Independent*, 17/09/2014, copyright © The Independent, 2014, www.independent.co.uk; Extract on page 75 adapted from "The next Labour leader must champion electoral reform" by Felix Ling, LabourList 09/07/2015, http://labourlist.org/2015/07/the-next-labour-leader-must-champion-electoral-reform/. Reproduced with permission; Extract on page 75 from "David Cameron: why keeping first past the post is vital for democracy", by David Cameron, *The Telegraph* 30/04/2011, copyright © Telegraph Media Group Limited 2011; An extract on page 97 about the Prison Radio Service, http://www.prisonradioassociation.org/about/, copyright © 2014 Prison Radio Association. Reproduced with permission; A quotation on page 98 by Anne Lewis. Used with kind permission; An extract on page 98 from Neighbourhood Watch, www.ourwatch.org.uk, copyright © NHWN, 2016. All rights reserved; Quote on page 100 by Besnik Vrapi in "Why are more students becoming special constables?" by Joanna Moorhead, *The Guardian*, 09/09/2013, copyright © Guardian News & Media Ltd 2016; Extract on page 102 from 'Youth courts need urgent reform, finds inquiry' by Neil Puffett, 19/06/2014, http://www.cypnow.co.uk/cyp/news/1144917/youth-courts-urgent-reform-inquiry, © MA Education 2016;The table on page 110 'Which organisations do people belong to?' adapted from *British Social Attitudes*, Vol 32, Politics, Table 1. Reproduced with permission of NatCen Social Research; An extract on page 122 about Scope, http://www.scope.org.uk/About-Us/What-We-Do. Reproduced with kind permission; Extract on page 122 about Stop HS2, http://stophs2.org/. Reproduced with kind permission; Table on page 133, average sales of daily newspapers in the UK, 2012, 2015. Source: Audit Bureau of Circulation, www.abc.org.uk; Quotation on page 142 from the Commonwealth Secretary General the Rt. Hon. Don McKinnon, London, 08/12/2005, copyright © Commonwealth Secretary, London, UK; An extract on page 144 from 'The education emergency facing Syria's children' by David Bull, 03/10/2013, UNICEF, https://blogs.unicef.org.uk/2013/10/03/the-education-emergency-facing-syrias-children. Reproduced with kind permission; An extract on page 155 from ShelterBox, http://www.shelterbox.org. Reproduced with kind permission; and Quotation on page 182 by Aimee Blackhouse from "Girl's race to save school", *The Manchester Evening News*, 17/04/2010, copyright © Mirrorpix, 2010.

Photograph acknowledgements:
p6tl Jacob Lund/Shutterstock, p6tr studioflara/Shutterstock, p6cl Oldham Chronicle, p6cr Alexander Raths/Shutterstock, p6bl Agencja Fotograficzna Caro/Alamy, p6br Debu55y/Shutterstock, p8tl Monkey Business Images/Shutterstock, p8tr Tommy (Louth)/Alamy, p8cl Ronnachai Palas/Shutterstock, p8c Zurijeta/Shutterstock, p8cr Natursports/Shutterstock, p8bl Iakov Filimonov/Shutterstock, p8br Janine Wiedel Photolibrary/Alamy, p12tr VOJTa Herout/Shutterstock, p12cl Angelo Ferraris/Shutterstock, p12cr Paul J Martin/Shutterstock, p12bl Sally and Richard Greenhill/Alamy, p12br Guy Somerset/Alamy, p13 Telegraph & Argus, Bradford, p14 bikeriderlondon/Shutterstock, p15 wronaphoto.com/Alamy, p16tr A and N photography/Shutterstock, p16l studioflara/Shutterstock, p16br Dave J Hogan/Getty Images, p18l Stasique/Shutterstock, p18c Image Source/Corbis, p18r Iakov Filimonov/Shutterstock, p19l Monkey Business Images/Shutterstock, p19r Djomas/Shutterstock, p21 © University of Essex, p22 Ace Stock Limited/Alamy, p23l Sipa Press/REX Shutterstock, p23r Blend Images/Alamy, p24 Commission for Racial Equality, p25 Stokkete/Shutterstock, p26t David Wootton/Alamy, p26b Oldham Chronicle, p27 Salena Grey, p28tl Georgiev/© UNICEF, p028tc Steven Clevenger/Corbis, p028tr Kljajo/© UNICEF, p28bl Lucinda Marland/Janine Wiedel Photolibrary/Alamy, p28br palash khan/Alamy, p29l Samir Bol /Anadolu Agency/Getty Images, p29r Sipa Press/REX Shutterstock, p30 CM Dixon/Print Collector/Getty Images, p31 Forance/Shutterstock, p32tl a katz/Shutterstock, p32tr Amy Johansson/Shutterstock, p32c © European Union, 1995–2016, p32bl Trevor Lush/Purestock/Alamy, p32br David Hartley/REX Shutterstock, p33l courtesy Aldbourne Youth Council www.4children.org.uk, p33r Thomas Ruffer/Agencja Fotograficzna Caro/Alamy, p34tl Bettmann/Corbis, p34tr Bettmann/Corbis, p34br Monkey Business Images/Shutterstock, p36tl Colorblind/Getty Images, p36tr Martin Jenkinson/Alamy, p36bl Neil McAllister/Alamy, p36br Alex Segre/Alamy, p38 iofoto/Shutterstock, p40 Visun Khankasem/Shutterstock, p41 Andrew Fox/Alamy, p42 Alex B. Huckle/GC Images/Getty Images, p43 James Steidl/Shutterstock, p44 courtesy Jenny Wales, p45l BasPhoto/Shutterstock, p45r Maggie Murray/Photofusion Picture Library/Alamy, p46 courtesy Jenny Wales, p48tl Elnur/Shutterstock, p48tr 10 Words/Shutterstock, p48bl Alexander Raths/Shutterstock, p48bc Debu55y/Shutterstock, p48br Monkey Business Images/Shutterstock, p54tl Strauss/Curtis/Corbis, p54tr Kiev.Victor/Shutterstock, p54cl © Scottish Parliamentary Corporate Body – 2012. Licensed under the Open Scottish Parliament Licence v1.0., p54cr Bob Davidson, p54b Clive Chilvers/Shutterstock, p56 courtesy Scott Mann MP, p57 copyright: British Youth Council, p58 Clive Chilvers/Shutterstock, p60 Strauss/Curtis/Corbis, p62 Bob Davidson, p63 PA Archive/PA Images, p64 Chris Montgomery/REX Shutterstock, p65 © UK Parliament/JessicaTaylor, p66tl nexus 7/Shutterstock, p66tr Richard Gardner/REX Shutterstock, p66bl photomak/Shutterstock, p66br goodluz/Shutterstock, p67 Kiev.Victor/Shutterstock, p68 © Scottish Parliamentary Corporate Body – 2012. Licensed under the Open Scottish Parliament Licence v2, p69 National Assembly for Wales Commission, p70 courtesy Jenny Wales, p71 Friends of Snibston, p72tl Kevin Peterson/Photodisc/Getty Images, p72tr Kevin Peterson/Photodisc/Getty Images, p72bl Kevin Peterson/Photodisc/Getty Images, p72br Barbara Penoyar/Photodisc/Getty Images, p78tl Pixellover RM 7/Alamy, p78tr Peter Dazeley/Photographer's Choice RF/Getty Images, p78cl Roger Bamber/Alamy, p78bl Justin Kase zfivez/Alamy, p78br Paul Doyle/Photofusion Picture Library/Alamy, p80bl Sally and Richard Greenhill/Alamy, p80br Graham M. Lawrence/Alamy, p82 DAI KUROKAWA/epa/Corbis, p83 Peter Dazeley/Photographer's Choice RF/Getty Images, p84tl Chris Jackson/Getty Images, p84tr Pixellover RM 7/Alamy, p84br Ben Pruchnie/Getty Images, p86 Sabphoto/Shutterstock, p90 Liverpool Echo Trinity Mirror, p91 Piotr Marcinski/Shutterstock, p92l Volodymyr Baleha/Shutterstock, p92r Stefano Cavoretto/Shutterstock, p93 Roger Bamber/Alamy, p94 Image Source/Getty Images, p95l stereoliar/Shutterstock, p95r stereoliar/Shutterstock, p96 Paul Doyle/Photofusion Picture Library/Alamy, p97 Prison Radio Association, p98 Annie Lewis, p99 Justin Kase zsixz/Alamy, p100t Sean Smith, p100cl bikeriderlondon/Shutterstock, p100cr Mark Harvey/Alamy, p100c ostill/Shutterstock, p100bl Mike Goldwater/Alamy, p100br Andrey Popov/Shutterstock, p101 Justin Kase zfivez/Alamy, p106tl Oscar Johns/Shutterstock, p106tr wellphoto/Shutterstock, p106c Jeff Gilbert/Alamy, p106bl Jim West/Alamy, p106br © Scope 2015, p108 G. K./Shutterstock, p109 grynold/Shutterstock, p110 Rawpixel.com/Shutterstock, p111 Oscar Johns/Shutterstock, p112 Colin Underhill/Alamy, p113t Jeff Gilbert/Alamy, p113b 10 Words/Shutterstock, p114 courtesy The SMASH Youth Project www.smash-youth-project.co.uk, p115 with thanks to Volunteering Matters and Deutsche Bank, p116l Zurijeta/Shutterstock, p116tl SpeedKingz/Shutterstock, p116tr SpeedKingz/Shutterstock, p116c SpeedKingz/Shutterstock, p116br Gelpi JM/Shutterstock, p117 © UK Parliament/Roger Harris, p118 AFP/Getty Images, p119 Twin Design/Shutterstock, p120 Fabrizio Bensch/Reuters, p121 Jim West/Alamy, p122tl © Scope 2015, p122tr © Scope 2015, p122b courtesy Stop HS2, p123 Johnny Greig/E+/Getty Images, p124 Simon Green, p125 Malcolm Case-Green/Alamy, p126tl Oleksiy Mark/Shutterstock, p126tr Volodymyr Krasyuk/Shutterstock, p126tcl Twin Design/Shutterstock, p126tcr Niloo/Shutterstock, p126bcl Pakhnyushchy/Shutterstock, p126bcr Stokkete/Shutterstock, p126b Richard Newton /Alamy, p128 Howard Burditt/Reuters, p129t Alexander Joe/AFP/Getty Images, p129b Alexander Demianchuk AS/AA/Reuters, p130 Norbert Michalke/imageBROKER/Alamy, p131 wellphoto/Shutterstock, p132l George Pimentel/WireImage/Getty Images, p132r Tim Rooke/REX Shutterstock, p132c Mark Pain/REX Shutterstock, p134t Steve Vidler/Alamy, p134b John Keeble/Getty Images, p135 Paul Davey/Demotix/Corbis, p136 public sector information licensed under the Open Government Licence v3.0, p137tl © Amnesty International 2015, p137bl © Anup Shah/Nature Picture Library, p137r courtesy Cure the NHS, p138 Mychele Daniau/AFP/Getty Images, p140t antpun/Shutterstock, p140b © European Union, 1995–2016, p141t courtesy United Communities, p141b Stewart Golf, p142l Veronica Garbutt/REX Shutterstock, p142r Mark Read/Camfed, p144 Unicef/2012/Schermbrucker, p146 UN, p147l United Nations Photo Library, p147r United Nations Photo Library, p147br Coalition to Stop the use of Child Soldiers, p148 photo by Staff Sgt. Fredrick Varney, p149 © Crown copyright, p150 Rawpixel.com/Shutterstock, p151 Paul Springett 06/Alamy, p152 JERRY LAMPEN/AFP/Getty Images, p153 Sipa Press/REX Shutterstock, p154 courtesy of PumpAid www.pumpaid.org, p155 ShelterBox - www.shelterbox.org, p156t Esiebo/© UNICEF, p156b Nathan Holland/Shutterstock, p157 © Crown copyright, p158 Gregg Vignal/Alamy, p162tl Wiltshire County Council Development Service for Young People, p162tr Tim Ockenden/PA Archive/PA Images, p162c Janine Wiedel/REX Shutterstock, p162c Janine Wiedel/Alamy, p162bl Jenny Wales, p162br courtesy the Young Co-operatives, p164 Wiltshire County Council Development Service for Young People, p165t courtesy Stoke-on-Trent City Council, p165b courtesy the Young Co-operatives, p166l bikeriderlondon/Shutterstock, p166r Pixsooz/Shutterstock, p166b public sector information licensed under the Open Government Licence v3.0, p167 Monkey Business Images/Shutterstock, p168t sakhorn/Shutterstock, p168bl Hriana/Shutterstock, p168br Samuel Borges Photography/Shutterstock, p169 dotshock/Shutterstock, p173 Monkey Business Images/Shutterstock, p176t diane555/iStockphoto, p176b courtesy Jenny Wales, p179 Amir Ridhwan/Shutterstock, p180 courtesy Jenny Wales, p181 David Hoffman/Photofusion, p182 Manchester Evening News, p183t Tim Ockenden/PA Archive/PA Images, p183b Tim Ockenden/PA Archive/PA Images.

Notes